PATHWAYS TO PARADISE

"So many women today are worried about their marriages, are unhappy with their relationships. They feel as if love has let them down. But love isn't an event. It's an experience. It requires the mutual investment of two people in one another and in their partnership. This book is about marriage, about relationships—about making love endure.

Couples *can* stay together and make love work. We can help."

Drs. Bonnie Maslin and Yehuda Nir

"...Very readable, beautifully constructed, and thoughtfully developed.... The case histories create an opportunity for laymen and professionals alike to understand much more about the workings of human interactions."

Paul Jay Fink, M.D.
President of The American
Psychiatric Association

Also by Bonnie Maslin, Ph.D.,
and Yehuda Nir, M.D.:

LOVING MEN FOR ALL THE RIGHT REASONS

NOT QUITE PARADISE

Making Marriage Work

Bonnie Maslin, Ph.D., and Yehuda Nir, M.D.

FAWCETT CREST • NEW YORK

A Fawcett Crest Book
Published by Ballantine Books
Copyright © 1987 by Bonnie Maslin and Yehuda Nir

Library of Congress Catalog Card Number: 86-6190

ISBN 0-449-21468-0

This edition published by arrangement with Doubleday & Company, Inc.

Manufactured in the United States of America

First Ballantine Books Edition: April 1988

To the children
Daniel, Aaron,
David & Sarah

ACKNOWLEDGMENTS

We gratefully acknowledge Juri Jurjevics, who not only gave us our first opportunity as authors, but offered us his continuing support and guidance on this work. Our thanks also to Themis Dimon, as always best friend and best critic. Her special wisdom helped shape this book. And thanks to Channa Taub, who can only be described as an extraordinary editor. And finally, our appreciation to Frieda Maslin, who doesn't have the word "no" in her vocabulary.

CONTENTS

AUTHORS' NOTE

The characters in this book are not real. Rather each is a composite developed from our years of clinical observation and research. Each couple represents our best effort to create a true picture in terms of psychological dynamics.

"My love to my husband was not only a matrimonial love, as betwixt man and wife, but a natural love, as the love of brethren, parents, and children, also a sympathetical love, as the love of friends, likewise a customary love, as the love of acquaintances, a loyal love, as the love of a subject, an obedient love, as the love to virtue, and uniting love, as the love of soul and body, a pious love, as the love to heaven, all which several loves did meet and intermix, making one mass of love."

— a seventeenth-century Englishwoman who was pining for her husband after he died

"In the seventeenth century maybe a woman could conceive of perfect love. But most women I know are in relationships that are not quite paradise."

— a twentieth-century American woman after reading the above

INTRODUCTION

❧ ❦

"Love is forever." At least, that's what you thought when you married your husband one bright June day, but now—six years later—you're wondering how you could have ever loved this man.

"All you need is love" seemed true when you and your man fell in love, but now that he's lost his job and your stepsons are living with you, you wonder if love is ever enough.

"Love makes the world go round" until you discovered that without a career of your own, the world seemed dull. But your husband wants you at home, to take care of him and the kids.

So many women today are worried about their marriages, are unhappy with their relationships. They feel as if love has let them down.

But love isn't an event. It's an experience. It requires the mutual investment of two people in each other and in their partnership. This book is about marriage, about relationships—about making them work, making love endure.

INTIMACY

We opened our first book, *Loving Men for All the Right Reasons*, with the thought that the capacity to achieve intimacy is central to a person's well-being. Today, we believe even more strongly in the importance of intimacy.

As therapists, we have devoted many years (over forty, between the two of us) to helping men and women gain new insights and find fresh solutions to their personal and marital problems. We have discovered that the key to happiness is making a serious commitment to another person. Why? Because intimacy is only possible in a committed and continuing relationship between two people.

Recently we visited close friends, Juri and Laurie, who had just welcomed home their first baby, Rosa. Over the course of the evening, Juri and Lauri took turns dancing with Rosa to the swing music drifting softly from the stereo. As we watched the calm descend over Rosa, we both were struck by the thought that from the beginning, the well-being of every person is forged in the intimacy of someone's arms.

THE INFIDELITY QUOTIENT

During infancy your very survival is in the hands of another person. It is through your sense of helplessness that you first develop the feeling of being valued by another being, and of valuing others. Out of this fact of your nature the need to be loved emerges. Your sense of well-being is nurtured within an intimate attachment.

But people do not stay the same forever. The passing of time changes us. Marriage changes us. And then the marriage itself changes. Is it inevitable that you will stop loving your man the way you once did, or that he will stop loving you? No. But if care is not taken, the love you and your man have for each other will erode, and this can threaten your relationship.

For a time, fashion suggested that love could thrive without exclusivity—that infidelity did not threaten a relationship. In our many years of practice, we have seen that for most couples, fidelity is a necessary ingredient for love to thrive, for the relationship to work. You must have trust and loyalty in your marriage. Relationships don't necessarily self-destruct with extramarital affairs. But you are fooling yourself if you believe that your relationship can grow when one partner's interest and loyalty is divided between two people.

Infidelity is a loss of faith and feeling in one's marriage. You may consider infidelity to be limited to the physical. And, yes, infidelity does include sexual infidelity—but it doesn't take just a physical affair to be unfaithful. Your body may remain faithful (out of habit, temperament, morality) long after you have ceased to care. There is also emotional infidelity, which takes many forms, but the result is that your marriage is lost to you as a source of pleasure and happiness. This loss leaves you vulnerable to a Mid-Marriage Crisis.

Frankly, once infidelity has reached crisis proportions, there is little to be done. But get to your relationship before this point of no return, and you *can* save it. You can make love endure.

That's the key: not only is a Mid-Marriage Crisis avoidable, but a good marriage can become a better one! Couples can stay together and make love work. We can help this happen for you.

HOW TO AVERT A MID-MARRIAGE CRISIS

We have developed a plan to help you understand your relationship, to help you make it work. This plan has four parts, each of which forms a section of this book.

I. Measuring Your Infidelity Quotient: The I.Q. Test

In this part of the book, you will bring the current state of your marriage into focus. What is it *really* like? How does it measure up? Is yours a marriage at risk? In order to enable you to make this sort of assessment, we've created the Infidelity Quotient Test to gauge the level of infidelity in your marriage. By completing the I.Q. Test and scoring yourself on the marital adjustment scale, you'll know where your relationship is going—before it gets there.

II. Identifying Your Marital Gridlock

It's not enough to know you're vulnerable; you need to understand why. The real reasons for your high I.Q. may be unclear or hidden. So if you've learned you may be headed for a Mid-Marriage Crisis, the only way to prevent it is by uncovering the source. There is a core conflict lurking behind every relationship in trouble. To discover this on your own is no easy task. But we're going to help you. In this part of the book, we describe eight couples who find themselves locked in relationships that simply aren't working, that aren't giving them what they need. These are eight of the most typical forms of marital gridlock. Somewhere among these, you will recognize your own. You can pinpoint the specific self-defeating patterns to which your marriage may have fallen prey. Is it possible to break the cycle? Yes—after you've uncovered its sources.

III. Can Your Marriage Be Saved?

You've been willing to acknowledge that your marriage is at risk. With hard work you've developed insight into the probable causes. This leads you to answer this twofold question: "Now that I know all this, do I *want* to make things better? And is it still possible, or is it too late?"

Can a good marriage be enhanced? Can a bad one be saved? Do you and your spouse have what it takes to turn things around? Do you want to? Is your marriage negotiable? Even the most difficult partnership can have strength and resilience. Learning whether these positive qualities exist requires knowing what to look for. This part of the book will guide you. You will find it challenging to be frank with yourself about your marriage's potential—but you will also find it rewarding. Because before you can strive to renew your marriage, you need to know that it stands a fighting chance.

IV. Negotiating a Loving Relationship: A New Language of Love

Can you really make your marriage better? Absolutely. It takes work, but your new understanding, your new insights into your marriage *can* be translated into action. In this final part of the book, we will help you learn to think, feel, and most importantly *communicate* differently with your spouse. Time and time again, we have seen that there is probably nothing that offers married couples a greater possibility of a happy future together than the capacity to truly communicate with each other. We want to put the capacity for real communication and emotional exchange within your grasp, so that yours will be a more gratifying and fulfilling marriage. We want to help you master a new "language of love."

IS THIS BOOK FOR YOU?

Not everyone with "marital problems" is married. Today, many people have long-lasting, exclusive relationships without marrying. In this book, you will often see the words *husband*, *wife*, and *spouse*. But you'll also see *partner*, *man*, and *mate*. This book is not for married people only. It is for those who are involved in a long-lasting, exclusive relationship—whether or not they are married. It is *not* for people in casual connections, in short-term relationships. If you are not married, we suggest that while you are reading this book, you regard the words *husband* and *wife* as substitutes for the word *partner*, and *marriage* as a substitute for *relationship*.

Is this book only for those people whose marriages are troubled? No. It is never too early to take a serious look at your relationship, to learn what makes it work and what may threaten it. Relationships must be nourished in order to thrive.

But if your relationship *is* troubled, this book can be a lifesaver. By picking up this book, you may be acknowl-

edging that you're a bit worried about your marriage—and
that is the first step to improving it!

Is this book for women only? Yes and no. Yes, because
it is addressed to women; no, because a man can gain
much insight about both his marriage and his wife by reading this book. But women are usually first to seek help for
a troubled marriage. This is not to suggest that it is a
woman's responsibility to repair a relationship. Both the
man and the woman are responsible for making their marriage work. But we can help you start the search for solutions, for understanding. Your efforts may not interest your
husband at first, but slowly but surely, he will want to
know what you're up to. Then you'll be able to work together to create a better marriage.

PART ONE

Measuring Your Infidelity Quotient (I.Q.)

"If I only knew then what I know now."

Who hasn't said these words? Who hasn't wished that life came packaged with a crystal ball? There are so many mistakes we might have avoided with the benefit of a little advance insight.

Fortunately most of us have more ability to see into the future than we might think. By taking a careful and thoughtful look at the present, we can forecast what's likely to come. This brings an enormous advantage: advance warning gives us the time and creates the opportunity to do things differently.

The basic purpose of the I.Q. Test is to forecast your marital future. The test contains fifty-five questions. Answering them will help you determine how your marriage is faring and what you can anticipate. After you complete the questionnaire and score each of your answers, you will discover your total—your Infidelity Quotient. This number will indicate if you seem bound in the direction of a Mid-Marriage Crisis. Your Infidelity Quotient is advance notice of what's to come.

This final score, while important, is not the only benefit of taking the I.Q. Test. In the answer keys, each question is accompanied by an explanation; the meanings behind the responses you make are provided. Each of these explanations will bring questions of your own to mind. The more it makes you reflect, consider, wonder, inquire, the greater the questionnaire's potential impact. It will arouse your curiosity about the way you love. Personal curiosity—the desire to know more and more—is the much-needed driving force behind your pursuit of change.

In order to create this I.Q. Test, a lot of heads were put together on your behalf. We drew upon our own clinical experience as therapists and consulted other noted professionals as well as respected scientific studies in the field of marital therapy. We interviewed married and divorced people. Above all, we tried to do what we do best: we listened so that you could hear what makes love work. Assessing your marriage is certain to be thought-provoking. Is it worth the challenge? Yes. Because it's a first step in the process of making a marriage better.

HOW TO TAKE THE I.Q. QUESTIONNAIRE

The questionnaire is designed as a whole unit. Actually many questions relate to one another. It is best to give yourself enough time to go through all fifty-five questions at one sitting.

Try not to take it when your emotions are running high —after the one great evening you've had together in six months, or in the stony silence after a big fight. The best assessment is done on a day that feels just like any other.

Attempt to be honest with yourself. Remember the advantage here is that *no one's looking*. Use this privacy. Let's face it—sometimes we're uncomfortable with our thoughts, particularly the unpleasant ones. We censor ourselves. Try to let your feelings and ideas surface unrestrainedly. You'll derive the most benefit by being spontaneous.

Above all it's worth remembering why knowing your I.Q. and averting a Mid-Marriage Crisis is so important to both you and your husband. In marriage no one person loses, no one person wins. There can be only two losers or two winners.

Directions

Sit down and give yourself enough time to go through all fifty-five questions. Don't rush. Remember: your honest answers will give you the best measure of your I.Q.! Once you've completed the questionnaire you can check your answers and compute your I.Q.

Not all questions will apply to you. If a question doesn't apply, write NA (no answer) beside it.* And have an extra piece of paper around since several questions require jotting down some notes.

*Note for women in long-lasting relationships but who are not married: Some of the questions apply to married people only. But many of the questions that use the terms *husband* or *marriage* can be answered by you. Again, we suggest that you consider those terms substitutes for *man*, *mate*, or *partner* and for *relationship* or *partnership*.

The Infidelity Quotient (I.Q.) Test

≫ ≪

MARITAL ADJUSTMENT

The first twenty-five questions explore the current state of your relationship—a gauge of how generally well-adjusted your marriage seems to be.

1. Off the top of your head list the things that satisfy you about your relationship. (Don't take more than a few moments to jot things down.) How many items are on your list?

   A. One
   B. Two
   C. Three
   D. Four
   E. More than four

2. Jot down a list of things that your man does that you don't like. How many items are on this list?

   A. One
   B. Two
   C. Three
   D. Four
   E. More than four

3. If you could do it all again would you

    A. marry the same person?
    B. marry a different person?
    C. not marry at all?
    D. just be friends?

4. How are your disagreements usually settled?

    A. You give in.
    B. Your man gives in.
    C. Mutual give and take.
    D. Nothing really gets resolved.

5. Circle any of the following that describe the way you've felt in the last six months.

    A. I don't have much of an appetite.
    B. Some days I feel so blue.
    C. I don't have the energy I used to have.
    D. I don't sleep very well.
    E. I've given up believing in the future.
    F. I wish my life were over.
    G. None of the above.

6. Does either of you threaten divorce? Or how many times has a conflict ended by one of you walking out on the other?

    A. Never
    B. Once
    C. Sometimes
    D. Frequently

7. Would you describe your man as a good friend?

    A. Yes
    B. No
    C. Maybe

8. Read over this list, then go back and check those factors you feel have caused *serious* difficulties in your relationship.

  ✓Lack of respect
  ✓Conflict over spending money

Religious differences
Political differences
✓Different interests
Different values
Absence of mutual friends
Unsatisfying sexual relationship
Constant bickering
Boredom
In-law problems
✓Having fallen out of love
Selfishness
✓Lack of cooperation
✓Infidelity
Conflict over having children
Financial lack of support
✓Emotional lack of support
Career conflict
Mistrust
Jealousy
Lazinesss
Humiliation
✓Disagreement over shared responsibilities
Lying
Criminal background
Unreliability
✓Communication problems
Others
Alcohol
Gambling
Drug abuse
Physical abuse
✓Emotional abuse
Sexual abuse

How many did you check?

A. None
B. One
C. Two
D. Three
E. Four or more

Did you check any of the last six factors?

AA. Yes
BB. No

9. Do you feel that any of the following are holding your marriage together?

   A. Religious pressure
   B. Fear of God
   C. Concern with what people will think
   D. Disappointment for the family
   E. Doubt of finding anyone else
   F. Fear the kids will hate you
   G. Fear of surviving on your own
   H. None of the above

10. Take a moment and think: How would you rate your marriage?

   A. Very happy
   B. Happy
   C. Average
   D. Unhappy
   E. Very unhappy

11. How would your partner rate your marriage?

   A. Very happy
   B. Happy
   C. Average
   D. Unhappy
   E. Very unhappy

12. Do you or your partner avoid each other?

   A. Often
   B. Sometimes
   C. Occasionally
   D. Never

(For the next eight questions the lettered lines represent a range of feelings you can have about each statement. For each question write down the letter that best reflects how you feel.)

13. My husband isn't as smart as I am.

Very true_____Not true at all
        A   B   C   D   E   F G

14. My husband appreciates me just as I am.

Very true_____Not true at all
        A   B   C   D   E F G

15. I can really talk with my husband about things that are important to me.

Very true_____Not true at all
        A   B   C   D   E F G

16. My marriage gives me enough opportunity to become the sort of person I'd like to be.

Very true_____Not true at all
        A   B   C   D   E F   G

17. My husband is affectionate toward me.

Very true_____Not true at all
        A   B   C   D   E   F G

18. In our house no one is afraid of saying what's on his or her mind.

Very true_____Not true at all
        A   B   C   D   E F G

19. We don't see eye to eye on many things.

Very true_____Not true at all
        A   B   C   D   E   F   G

20. Our marriage is a give-and-take partnership.

Very true_____Not true at all
        A   B   C   D   E   F G

21. Rank the following in terms of importance to your spouse.

    2 Work   8 Television   10 Religion
    5 You   3 Marriage   11 Friends
    1 Children   7 Parents   9 Power
    12 Sports   6 Money   4 Love

    You are:

    A. #1
    B. #2
    C. #3
    D. #4
    E. Below #4

22. Which comes closest to your thoughts?

    A. I stay for the sake of my children.
    B. If I didn't have children, things might be different.
    C. I don't argue with my husband because of the children.
    D. I weigh my happiness against the children's happiness.
    E. I'm afraid of the effect our relationship has on the kids.
    F. I'm not particularly worried about my children.

23. Are any of these feelings part of the current emotional climate of your marriage?

    A. Too much water under the bridge.
    B. Useless.
    C. Hopeless.
    D. We're better off apart.
    E. I can't wait to get out.
    F. It wasn't meant to be.
    G. I don't give a damn.
    H. It's not a good marriage, but it's not that bad either.

24. Do any of the following describe your feelings? Choose one that comes closest to your sentiments.

A. I'm fed up.
B. My feelings are dead.
C. I can't forgive him.
D. I hate him.
E. He makes me sick.
F. We have our problems.

25. Are any of these your conclusions? Select one that best reflects your feelings.

A. A relationship isn't in the stars for me.
B. It's his problem.
C. All men are bastards.
D. Men can't be trusted.
E. Men are out for themselves.
F. I like my husband—I just wish he were a little different.

MARITAL ADJUSTMENT ANSWER KEY

1. A relationship can withstand life's stress if it's anchored in a basic sense of satisfaction. If you can't really bring that feeling into view, your marriage may be slipping off this important foundation. Score 2 points for A or B. Add 1 point if it took you more than a few moments to come up with an idea.

2. Surprisingly *what* you don't like isn't the key issue—it's *how much* about him you don't like that can spell trouble. Score 2 points for C, D, or E.

3. The feeling that you are stuck with the wrong man is obviously a problem. Score 2 points for B. But bitter feelings that make you want to renounce the institution of marriage are also a bad sign. Score 3 points for C. And the feelings of wanting to be just friends often implies that a marriage lacks romance and excitement. Score 2 points for D.

4. A sense that *you* give in may be a sign that you feel powerless, and, more often than not, resentful. (In contrast, women who check B feel it's a sign of compatibility with their mates.) Score 2 points for A. Unresolved disagreements always resurface, sooner or later; dissension is a sign of difficulty. Score 2 points for D.

5. Everyone has his or her bad days. But if you've checked several of these descriptions and they're persistent you may be struggling with feelings of depression. It may not be your marriage alone that's causing these feelings; nonetheless, depression and marital difficulties are frequently associated. Score 2 points for A through F. If you checked three or more choices, add 2 points. (If your life seems to have ground to a halt under the weight of these sorts of feelings, professional help is essential—no matter what the state of your marriage.)

6. In the heat of argument, we may lash out and say things we soon regret. But threatening to leave, and acting it out (even if it's only running off overnight to a friend's house) are critical signals. Score 3 points for D. Score 2 points for C. If once, five years ago, you threatened divorce, forget it.

7. A sentiment that seems ubiquitous among women who are "happily" married is that a spouse is a valued friend. Not feeling that sort of connection may be problematic. Score 2 points for B. Score 1 point for C.

8. If you've checked three or more areas, the fabric of your relationship is likely to be riddled with problems. Score 3 points for D or E. Addictions and/or abuse (the last six items on the list) are in and of themselves *very* significant indicators. Add another 10 points for addictions and/or abuse. But, more importantly, if you checked AA, please be

aware that your relationship must get professional help.

9. Fear is the common denominator in these answers. Such tension interferes enormously with marital well-being. Score 2 points for A through G.

10. Taking time to think about your marriage may enable you to gain perspective. The feeling in your heart that you are unhappy is an indisputable measure of marital discord—even if you can't pinpoint how or why things are bad. Score 2 points for D or E.

11. In the rush of your life, you may not give thought to the satisfaction your partner does or doesn't derive from your union. If he's unhappy, discord may arise—even if things are okay with you. Score 2 points for D or E.

12. Chronic avoidance—you or he spend more and more time at the bar, the office, the golf club, Mother's—spells trouble. Score 3 points for A; score 2 points for B.

13. Agreeing with this sentiment in the extreme may be a way of expressing lack of respect—a corrosive element in a relationship. Score 3 points for A or B; one point for C.

14. Marriage doesn't have to be a mutual admiration society, but feeling valued is associated with good marital adjustment. Score 2 points for G. Score 1 point for E or F.

15. Good communication is essential for a good marriage. Score 3 points for F or G; one point for E.

16. Happy couples feel that a good marriage is a place that supports and encourages personal growth. Feeling stifled bodes badly for marital accord. Score 3 points for F or G.

17. The total absence of some form of physical de-
    monstrativeness is frequently associated with dis-
    cord. Score 3 points for G. A sense that there isn't
    enough TLC can eventually create frustration.
    Score 2 points for E or F.

18. Democracy isn't just the best form of government.
    It's the best basis for a marriage. A marriage must
    have a forum for debate. Score 3 points for F or
    G, and 1 point for E.

19. This doesn't mean marriages between Democrats
    and Republicans are automatically headed for the
    rocks. Rather, constant lack of agreement may
    mean an absence of shared values, which can raise
    problems. Score 2 points for A or B.

20. Marital well-being is marked by feelings of mutu-
    ality and reciprocity. If you give and he takes, or
    vice versa, your marriage may be dangerously off-
    balance. Score 3 points for F or G. If you feel put
    upon, even slightly, problems may be brewing.
    Score 2 points for E.

21. If you're not #1 or #2, you are likely to feel
    frustrated with the priorities in your spouse's life.
    Score 2 points for C, D, or E.

22. If kids are weighing on your mind, chances are
    your marriage is under strain. Score 2 points for A
    through E.

23. Overwhelming resignation is an admission of
    hopelessness. It's a serious and troubling sign.
    Score 3 points for A through G.

24. Remember, the mere presence of frustration
    doesn't doom a connection. Anger may mean we
    still care to get mad. It is unrelenting bitterness
    and deeply ingrained disgust that rupture bonds.
    Score 3 points for A through E.

25. If you feel victimized by your partner, if you're at a stage where you externalize responsibility, you may be on the path to marital disaster. Score 3 points for A through E.

Scoring

Add up the points you've gotten so far. This is your Marital Adjustment Score. Enter it on the line marked Marital Adjustment Score on page 33. Then go on to the second section.

SEXUAL ADJUSTMENT

The next fifteen questions focus on sex. This part of the assessment will help you evaluate how sexually well adjusted your marriage is.

1. Circle any of the following that describe your sexual encounters with your husband.

   A. We make up in bed.
   B. I want to be held; he wants to go to sleep.
   C. He watches TV till all hours.
   D. I'm always afraid the kids will walk in on us.
   E. I'm embarrassed to show him what makes me feel good.
   F. He's wham-bam-thank-you-ma'am.
   G. It's part of our lives.
   H. I'm usually too tired to enjoy it.
   I. We sleep in separate beds.
   J. He's got weird ideas about sex.
   K. We have a pact not to go to bed angry.

2. Your husband accuses you of being interested in other men.

   A. Always
   B. Sometimes
   C. Rarely
   D. Never

3. Select a statement that best describes sexual functioning in your relationship.

    A. I've never had an orgasm.
    B. I used to have orgasms.
    C. I pretend to have orgasms.
    D. I generally have orgasms.
    E. I would have orgasms but my husband doesn't spend enough time at it.
    F. We both have orgasms.
    G. He's become impotent.

4. How often do you or your partner refuse sex?

    A. Always
    B. Frequently
    C. Sometimes
    D. Rarely
    E. Never

5. Do you wish you had more sex, but your husband rejects your advances?

    A. Yes
    B. No

6. Which statement best describes your sexual fantasies?

    A. My sexual fantasies are a complement to my sex life.
    B. My sexual fantasies are more exciting than my sex life.
    C. My sexual fantasies are more important to me than sex with my partner.
    D. My sexual fantasies are a substitute for sex with my partner.
    E. I never have sexual fantasies.

7. Choose a statement that describes your sexual relations.

    A. I'd rather satisfy myself than have sex with him.
    B. I know he masturbates.

C. Since I've been married I masturbate only occasionally.

D. My husband enjoys watching me masturbate.

8. Which statement best describes your feelings about having sex with someone other than your partner?

A. I've never had an affair.

B. I had a fleeting affair.

C. I'm just waiting for one to happen.

D. I wish I had the guts to do it.

E. I haven't been able to feel the same about my husband since.

9. How would you rate your partner's interest in sex compared to your own?

A. Much less

B. About the same

C. Much more

10. Which of the following may be true for you?

A. I suspect my husband has had (or is having) homosexual relations.

B. I've had homosexual relations.

C. I've had fantasies or dreams about homosexual lovemaking.

D. When I was younger I had sex play (playing doctor, mutual masturbation, petting, kissing) with a girlfriend.

E. I've never given a thought to homosexuality.

11. Which sentiments seem closest to your own?

A. I can't stand to be touched by him.

B. I pretend to be asleep when he comes into bed.

C. I'm relieved when he's not interested.

D. I can't bring myself to make love with him.

E. I do it but I don't enjoy it.

F. He's a good lover.

G. I go through the motions.

12. The only good thing we have going is sex.

    A. Yes
    B. No

13. Are any of these close to your feelings?

    A. He's a good husband but I dread having sex.
    B. I like him but I don't love him.
    C. I love him but I don't like him.
    D He's nice but he doesn't turn me on.
    E. He turns me on but I'm not sure how much I
       love him.
    F. I look forward to making love with him.

14. Sometimes I think I wouldn't mind if my husband
    would have sex with someone else. Maybe he
    wouldn't pressure me.

    A. My thought exactly.
    B. An occasional idea.
    C. Never crossed my mind.

15. Which is true for you after sex?

    A. We both are silent.
    B. I want to talk but he doesn't.
    C. We chat a bit.
    D. We have some of our most important conver-
       sations.

SEXUAL ADJUSTMENT ANSWER KEY

1. The bed may be the first place where problems
   show up. It may reflect a breakfown in communication (C, E, F, I, J) or differences in needs (B, D,
   H). Score 2 points for B, C, D, E, F, H, I, or J. If
   bed is a cozy place to kiss and make up (A), don't
   score. Unless, however, you are making up in the
   wake of abusive behavior. Score 2 points if Answer A happens under these circumstances.

2. Consistent accusations are often part of turbulent periods in marriage. Score 2 points for A or B. Even if you are "innocent," score this. Part of the problem may stem from your wanting him to be in doubt.

3. The presence or absence of orgasms is not as important as a *loss* of the capacity to experience sexual climax with the same partner. Score 2 points for B or G. Also the feelings of being denied pleasure by a partner, or the need to deny an absence of pleasure to a partner may be a telltale measure of how isolated you feel. Score 2 points for C or E. No one has to be a gold-medal sexual gymnast —but good sex is a good sign.

4. Boredom, disgust, and bitterness are often behind consistent sexual rejection. Score 2 points for A or B. But always saying yes has its own difficulties. If you can't say no, you may feel frightened and/ or powerless. Sexual intimidation is a troubling sign. Score 2 points for E.

5. Marriage is not courtship. The frequency of intercourse invariably diminishes and levels off. However, if you wish you had more sex and your husband seems to avoid, disregard, or reject your advances, trouble is brewing. Score 2 points for A.

6. Fantasies can be fantastic. Most people, even the most "well-adjusted," dream of others. Enjoy your dreams—unless they've become obstacles to pleasure with your own partner or have become substitutes for the real thing. Score 2 points for C or D.

7. Score 2 points for A or B. This isn't a judgment about masturbation but rather about dissatisfaction. This withdrawal into the self may hint at a loss of hope in the possibility of *mutual* satisfaction.

8. A large percentage of married women have extra-marital affairs. Marriages don't necessarily self-destruct in the wake of an affair. But a drive toward other people, a *need* for an affair, may hint at a growing marital rift. Score 2 points for C, D, or E.

9. It's not quantity of desire; it's compatibility of desire that's a key to marital accord. A wide disparity in either direction suggests discord. Score 2 points for A or C.

10. No one is certain about all the variables that affect our gender identity and sexual preference. But most studies suggest that homoerotic play in childhood or dreams in adulthood are so common that they aren't significant indicators. But if as adults we find ourselves acting on our homoerotic feelings, it may indicate that we are struggling with a sense of our sexual self. This behavior is often an unshared secret, which can create further conflict. Score 2 points for A or B.

11. Physical revulsion, disgust, or even boredom are closely connected to angry disappointment with a spouse. If you are repelled, you are probably enraged. Yours is a partnership in serious trouble. Score 2 points for everything except F.

12. Sex isn't glue; it can't hold a marriage together. A physical union can't erase an emotional rift. Score 2 points for A.

13. To be caught in contradictory feelings is a sign of a brewing conflict. Something is creating this confusion. Score 2 points for A through E.

14. If you want him off your back and out of your bed things are shaky. If you want to be left alone you may eventually find yourself left alone. Score 2 points for A or 1 point for B.

15. Lack of communication in or out of bed makes a marriage vulnerable. Score 2 points for A or B.

Scoring

Add up the points in this second section for your Sexual Adjustment Score. Put that number on the line marked Sexual Adjustment Score on page 33. Then, go on to the next section.

PREMARITAL ADJUSTMENT

The next fifteen questions don't address your current situation. The emphasis here is on how things were before you were married: a look at premarital adjustment.

1. How does your mother view your marriage? Your husband?

   A. She approves.
   B. She has no strong feelings.
   C. She isn't happy.
   D. She disapproves.

2. The day you got married you

   A. had the jitters.
   B. knew it was a mistake.
   C. had second thoughts.
   D. felt eager and excited.

3. If most people rate childhood as happy, how would you rate yours?

   A. Very happy
   B. Happy
   C. Okay
   D. Unhappy
   E. Miserable

4. How would you rate your conficts with your parents?

A. None
B. Few
C. Some
D. Frequent
E. Constant

5. With how many people did you have sexual relations before marriage?

A. I was a virgin.
B. I had sex but only with my spouse.
C. I had sex with someone other than my spouse.
D. I had sex with others.

6. How long have you been married?

A. One to five years
B. Six to ten years
C. Eleven to fifteen years
D. Sixteen to twenty-five years

7. How much time was there between the time you decided to marry until the date of your marriage?

A. Less than one month
B. One to three months
C. Three to six months
D. More than six months

8. Did you have repeated disagreement, conflict, and/or dissension before marriage?

A. Always
B. Frequently
C. Sometimes
D. Rarely
E. Never

9. Were you pregnant before being married?

A. Yes.
B. No.
C. Yes, it was planned.

10. How old were you when you married?

    A. Under eighteen
    B. Nineteen to twenty-three
    C. Twenty-four to twenty-nine
    D. Thirty to forty
    E. Over forty

11. Are your parents divorced?

    A. Yes, when I was a child.
    B. Yes, when I was a teenager.
    C. No.

12. How many times have you, and how many times has your husband, been divorced? (Choose an answer for each of you.)

    A. Once
    B. Twice
    C. Three Times
    D. Never

13. Consider the disappointments, complaints, and disillusionments you have about your husband. How do they compare to the way you've felt in earlier relationships?

    A. Identical
    B. Very similar
    C. Similar
    D. Different

14. Think of the character traits and personality problems that you consider most objectionable in your spouse. Could any of the following be true?

    A. My father was like that.
    B. My brother was like that.
    C. My mother was like that.
    D. My mother thought my father was like that.
    E. It reminds me of my family.
    F. It's not reminiscent of anyone I'm close to.

15. How would you rate your parents' marriage?

A. Perfect
B. Good
C. Average
D. Unhappy
E. Miserable

PREMARITAL ADJUSTMENT ANSWER KEY

1. A wife is always a daughter. This relationship predates (and may postdate) a marriage—don't minimize its significance. If you bucked strong parental opposition in marrying, beware. Once the glow is gone from a relationship, you may find yourself agreeing with the very opinions you rejected. Why? You may fight it, but those judgments gnaw at you, often coloring your vision of your spouse. Score 2 points for C or D.

2. Don't ignore your instincts when they are strongly felt. Many couples in trouble admit to serious misgivings from day one. Score 2 points for B or 1 point for C.

3. There is nothing that creates greater havoc in a marriage than bringing along the unfinished business of childhood. You may end up looking for solace you never had, which creates enormous pressure for your spouse. Score 2 points for D or E.

4. Becoming a separate, mature individual—the best material for marital success—means breaking away from one's parents. This has to include some head-on collisions with them. If you were a Goody Two-shoes, you may have lacked the courage to break away. Or, if you were the wildest kid on the block, you may have been too angry and destructive to find yourself. Such extremes may have prevented you from finding self-definition. Score 2 points for A, D, or E.

5. If you were a nice girl and *didn't*, you may grow into a woman who wished she had. Ironically, premarital celibacy leaves some women vulnerable to marital discontent. Score 2 points for A or B.

6. Forty to fifty percent of marriages of women in their twenties end in divorce. For those women married in their thirties the rates are even higher. So while marriage is still universal (nine out of ten people in the United States still marry) it is hardly till death do us part. The point: As soon as any of us marry we have a built-in divorce probability factor. Score 2 points for just being married.

7. The time from making the decision to actually taking the plunge is a useful period, a chance to see how the prospect of commitment makes you *both* feel. Depriving yourself of this initial "getting to know you" period may mean problems will surface when things get considerably more complicated. Score 2 points for A or B.

8. Unresolved, recurrent problems are a significant indicator of future discord. Once a pattern is established, its repetition erodes the bonds between two people. Score 2 points for A or B.

9. Pressure? Regrets? Resentment? Whatever is operating emotionally, the statistics aren't in your favor. Unplanned premarital pregnancy makes you prone to disharmony to the breaking point. Score 2 points for A.

10. The picture isn't rosy for women who marry before age eighteen: the divorce rate is two times that of the general population. Why does early marriage create a particular risk for women? Deferring personal growth while taking on the demands of caretaking hinder a young woman's development of a sense of who she is. What's the risk? The identity that eventually emerges may not be compatible with that of the man she married. Score 2 points for A.

11. First the good news. Children of divorce are not turned off to marriage. On the contrary, they have a determination to make things work. Unfortunately, if your parents are divorced you are more likely to find yourself contending with the same situation. Score 2 points for A or B.

12. Having a record of failures may mean that you or your spouse are caught in a self-defeating style of relating. The greatest danger is that this pattern will repeat and disrupt your current marriage. Score 2 points for B or C. If you or he have a history of repeated breakups without the benefit of marriage, give yourself a score too. If both partners have this sort of track record, double the score. Yours is a high-risk marriage.

13. If there is a recurrent theme to your dissatisfactions with men, you may be caught in a pattern, which makes the possibility of marital crisis more probable. Score 2 points for A, B, or C.

14. Whether you've found somene who *is* similar to an early, important, negative figure in your life, or whether you just perceive him as such, you may be reliving childhood conflicts in your adult relationship. Score 2 points for A through E.

15. Happily married parents provide a good model. Growing up in an embattled or unhappy home doesn't offer this support. Score 2 points for D or E. Ironically, a house without dissension can also be a confusing model, burdening you with unrealistic expectations. Therefore, score 2 points for A.

Scoring

Add the points to get your third and last subscore, your Premarital Adjustment Score. Enter this value on the line marked Premarital Adjustment Score.

Marital Adjustment Score _____58_____
Sexual Adjustment Score _____3_____
Premarital Adjustment Score _____8_____

Add the three scores together. The total value is your Infidelity Quotient.

INTERPRETING YOUR SCORE 68

Your Infidelity Quotient is a tool. Its purpose is to reveal the state of your marriage. We've found that a total I.Q. of 40 or more generally indicates a relationship that warrants attention. In order to score that total, you had to identify with many troubling issues.

Every time you scored an answer, you were acknowledging that a problem exists. Think of your I.Q. as a frank appraisal of what's going on in your marriage. All of us wonder about our partnerships, but being able to literally "add it all up" gives you the total picture in a tangible way. Your I.Q. is a concrete index of whether your marriage is healthy or whether it is moving beyond a tolerable level of difficulty.

Your total I.Q. isn't the only score that deserves attention. Having either a Marital Adjustment Score above 20 or a Sexual Adjustment Score above 15 is worrisome. Sometimes marriages are troubled in select or narrow areas. Problems may not yet have seeped into all areas of your life together. It's important not to be lulled into thinking, "Gee, things really are okay except for. . ."A subscore may bring potential problems into relief. But marriages don't fall apart overnight. Even in the rare instances when they seem to—perhaps under the stress of death, illness, or some other sudden trauma—it's likely that a difficult life event has pushed a couple's already high I.Q. beyond a tolerable level. And a marriage with only a few problem areas stands the greatest chance for improvement.

The most useful way to interpret your results is by asking yourself: "How did these questions make me feel?" Even if your score did *not* achieve the critical thresholds we've established, did anything arouse your interest and concern about your marriage? Did you hear yourself say, "That's me," "That's us"? It's never too early to pay attention to a relationship. The best time to avert crisis is as early as possible—as soon as you get an indication.

A word about your Premarital Adjustment Score. Unlike the Marital Adjustment and the Sexual Adjustment scores, these questions don't evaluate how well your marriage is currently faring. They are concerned with some of the circumstances, events, and attitudes that preceded your marriage. Some people come to marriage with an above-average predisposition for marital discord. Their marriages are more vulnerable than others. So a Premarital Adjustment Score above 15 deserves attention. It may indicate that your marriage has a built-in *potential* for trouble— even though it may not feel troubled as yet.

NOW WHAT?

Now that you have answered the questions in the I.Q. Test and perhaps found yourself with a high score, your concern has probably been aroused. It is not a comfortable feeling. It shouldn't be: comfort makes us complacent, and complacent people are neither curious nor interested in change. If your high I.Q. disturbs you, you're on your way to a better marriage. Discomfort is the cutting edge of change. It leaves you curious, wondering why your marriage may be on a troubled path. It generates more questions: "Why do I have a high I.Q.?" "Where does it come from?" Learning these answers is the next stage in averting a Mid-Marriage Crisis.

PART TWO

Marital Gridlock*: Eight Couples in Conflict

The test you just completed is the yardstick against which you can measure your marriage. A high I.Q. puts you on notice; it warns you that something may be wrong. Now you must ask yourself, "What is the cause; what accounts for my high I.Q.?"

Behind every relationship with active, or potential, problems lies a hidden, predictable, and repetitive pattern of conflict. Each day your marital problems may *feel* different: the content of your disputes may vary; your arguments may seem unique; your complaints to and about each other may sound new. Yet at the heart of your discontent— like that of every other couple in conflict—is an inflexible cycle. An inflexible cycle guarantees trouble because rigidity and predictability eventually doom any relationship. Intimacy, commitment, and love flourish when a marriage is dynamic, when a man and woman are flexible, adaptable, responsive, spontaneous. When a couple loses these qualities, we say they are in Marital Gridlock. They have lost their potential for growth.

Marital Gridlock *is* reversible. You can break out of your Marital Gridlock by uncovering and identifying your hidden pattern. The key word here is *hidden*. A cycle of conflict is not easy to discern. To help you identify your hidden pattern, we are going to offer eight of the most typical patterns of couples trapped in Marital Gridlock.

Quite possibly, you are unaware that there are typical patterns to the way couples conflict, one with the other. You may feel that each person is unique, an individual unlike any other. Yes, each person *is* different, but there are also many ways in which we all resemble one another. These similarities surface in the way couples relate. Despite the endless variety of people, there are only a limited number of patterns typical of couples in conflict. We don't maintain that our eight scenarios encompass every potential marriage conflict. But most types of conflicts that we've seen are at least partially represented in these eight scenarios.

The first of the eight couples you will encounter, Cindy and Anthony, are caught in a pattern. Could it be yours? At first glance, their situation may seem quite different from yours. But look below the surface, and you may discover that you are contending with many of the very same issues. And rest assured, if their pattern doesn't strike a responsive chord, another will.* As you move from pattern to pattern, you will move closer and closer to discovering the one that is yours.

A note of caution. No doubt there will be some people who won't find themselves and their marriage anywhere in the pages that follow. If you are one of those people, remember that if you have a high I.Q. it's no accident. You have a pattern, but perhaps you're not ready to acknowledge it. This often happens. For example, if things have, for the moment, gotten better between you and your partner, it's particularly difficult for you to acknowledge that you and your partner are in conflict. Ironically, things have to get worse for some couples before they're willing to try to make them better. Understand, when that moment comes, that help is at hand—right here in this book!

CINDY and ANTHONY:
Beauty and the Beast

⤜ ⤛

Cindy waited only until Anthony pulled the car out of her parents' driveway. "Mother puts out the good linen and Grandma's crystal, she polishes every piece of silver herself, and you have to have your can of Coke on the table. This isn't your family; it's mine. I don't ask you to love my mother—just be civil to her. But no! Not you! You go out of your way to offend her. Did you see her face when you drank from that can? Couldn't there be one Thanksgiving dinner where you let up?"

Cindy knew the answer before she finished the question. From day one, the chemistry between Anthony and her mother had been clear—instant dislike. Cindy knew her mother was prim and proper (Anthony dubbed her Mrs. P.—as in a Perfect Pain). And even though Anthony's family were loud and showy, it had never prevented Cindy from loving them. Couldn't her husband find it in himself to be nice, to humor her mother? "If I hadn't grabbed Mother in the kitchen and told her how happy we were to be with the family, you would have succeeded in ruining the whole day. And what really drives me up a wall is that even though I drag you here kicking and screaming, you like it. Not that you'd dare admit it."

Typically, Anthony didn't respond. Cindy knew that the two-hour ride home would be silent and icy. A lump grew in her throat. She felt hot tears rising and shook her head.

41

Why? Why? Why? Why does this always have to happen? If it isn't family, it's friends. Friends? He could even fight with a boss, or a cab driver, or anyone.

Cindy knew Anthony wasn't an easy man. Her best friend, Jennifer, had been blunt from the beginning. "He's trouble. You two are day and night; you're crazy to go after this relationship." But Cindy had seen something behind Anthony's gruff exterior. Still, at times like this, getting at that goodness seemed impossible.

The ride was just as she expected. When they finally arrived home, Anthony stormed around the house. Cindy debated how to ride out his fury: Read in the bedroom? Go next door to Joan's house for coffee? She picked up the phone, hoping that Joan would insist she drop by. On the third ring Anthony stormed into the kitchen and all hell broke loose. "You can't wait fifteen minutes before you start on the phone. And who told you I wanted my closet straightened out? I can't find a damn thing now. I'm sick and tired of your putting things away before I've even had a chance to use them. Why can't you get off my back? Half the time you leave everything up to me; the other half you want to run my life." The phone clicked and Joan's voice chimed, "Oh, Cindy, it's you. I can hear the madman in the background. Should I come over? I'm not afraid to tell him off."

Thank God it was Joan. Cindy didn't have to go through a charade to explain about the shouting. With some friends she'd run out of excuses for Anthony's behavior. It was a relief that Joan knew a lot, though there was plenty more that Cindy couldn't bear to reveal. Joan could be so blunt. Cindy sometimes wondered whether Joan wasn't too pushy. It was a wonder their friendship had lasted this long, but Joan was her next-door neighbor and very persistent about their friendship. "I'm coming—ready or not," Joan warned as she hung up.

The knock on the door had its desired effect. Anthony retreated to the bedroom, tossing a pencil and pad at Cindy. "Here, you and Joan can tally up my bad points together. Have a good time." Joan entered shaking her head, "I see the beast has retreated. Poor beauty; you look like a wounded puppy. Let's have a glass of wine and talk about anything but men. Did you straighten out that rent increase our landlord dumped on you? The crook. These garden apartments are anything but Eden. I can never figure out why you two stay put. Your husband makes more in a month than I do in a year. Aren't you even looking for your own house?"

Oh God, thought Cindy. How can I tell her that Anthony refuses to go house hunting. She lied, "I think we'd both rather wait till we have a family before we make the move."

"And the rent hike," Joan repeated. "You're going to swallow that whole?"

"Actually," Cindy answered, "Tony did have it out with the landlord. I'm glad I wasn't around to hear the conversation, but Mr. Jager did lower the increase a bit."

Joan laughed, "Cindy, you're incredible. Anthony may not be the white knight, but, boy, does he do battle for you. I don't think the two of you would survive a day without each other. You'd melt and he'd turn to stone. You're a perfect pair—a match made in someone's strange vision of heaven."

Before she could think it, Joan articulated Cindy's thoughts. "I can read that look on your face. 'I never want to see this bigmouthed so-called friend again.' Take it easy. I love you, toots. Even though being best friends with an angel can be such a strain. And you love me the way you love Anthony—in spite of our miserable selves." Joan made a ridiculous face. Cindy smiled, then laughed. Her bigmouthed friend was right. Unfortunately, with her husband it was hardly a laughing matter.

DISCERNING THE PATTERN OF CONFLICT

Although we are all individuals, there are basic similarities in all of us—and in all our marriages. In most marriages, a predictable sequence of conflicts can be uncovered.

The basis for Cindy and Anthony's conflict seems easy to spot. Anthony practically admits that he's a "difficult man." Cindy seems to be doing her best to smooth over the rough edges of her relationship and of her man. It would be easy to conclude that Anthony requires a crash course in manners and Cindy a pat on the back. You might even think that Cindy, who is such a nice person, should get rid of Anthony and find herself a decent man for a change. But don't be deceived into thinking that Cindy is Beauty and Anthony the Beast. The key to discerning a conflict is to look beyond the obvious.

Each person brings a Wish to a relationship. It's a recognized conscious desire, the answer to the question, "What do I want from my marriage?" However, the conscious wish is influenced by each person's unconscious Need. The continual friction between a couple has its source in the collision of their needs. Therefore, in order to break Marital Gridlock it is essential to unearth the unconscious needs.

Let's look more carefully at Cindy and Anthony. Although Cindy is unclear about what she wants from her marriage, she has one simple wish—that her marriage should be considerably more pleasant than it is now. "I wish I knew what I want—but it's not what I have now." Anthony's wish is more precise: marriage can be hassle-free only if it is unencumbered—a union strictly between two people. As he puts it, "I'd like to be married and then move a thousand miles from anyone either of us know. On a desert island I'd be a great husband."

Now let's take a look at their needs. (We will state them here, but in the course of this chapter, as you read about Anthony's and Cindy's pasts, you will learn how we uncovered these needs.) It may surprise you to learn that Cindy is an angry person—an angry person who cannot acknowledge her angry feelings. Her unconscious need is to avoid and disown her anger. And rough, tough Anthony? Anthony is a man who feels like a vulnerable little boy. He has an inner core of pain that leaves him feeling vulnerable. His unconscious need is to protect himself.

Their stormy relationship serves their needs perfectly. Although Cindy complains about Anthony's temper, rudeness, and hostility, his behavior suits her unconscious need: Anthony becomes the spokesperson for the feelings of

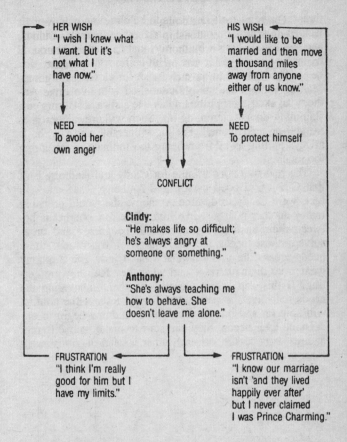

HER WISH
"I wish I knew what
I want. But it's
not what I
have now."

HIS WISH
"I would like to be
married and then move
a thousand miles
away from anyone
either of us know."

NEED
To avoid her
own anger

NEED
To protect himself

CONFLICT

Cindy:
"He makes life so difficult;
he's always angry at
someone or something."

Anthony:
"She's always teaching me
how to behave. She
doesn't leave me alone."

FRUSTRATION
"I think I'm really
good for him but I
have my limits."

FRUSTRATION
"I know our marriage
isn't 'and they lived
happily ever after'
but I never claimed
I was Prince Charming."

anger Cindy is unwilling to call her own. With Anthony around to be the bad guy, Cindy is reassured that she is the good guy in their relationship. And though Cindy says her wish is for a peaceful relationship, she unconsciously fears it. In the quiet and still of such a relationship, she would hear the intolerable and unacceptable voice of her own angry feelings.

Anthony's need to protect himself is also served by their marriage. He protects himself by shielding himself from closeness. At arm's distance, Cindy is less of an emotional threat. Anthony feels he wants to be close; he blames their lack of closeness on outside interference (parents, friends, and so forth). That's why he says that he wishes they could be married and live far away. But he fails to recognize that he is afraid, afraid to have his wish for closeness fulfilled. Making Cindy continually dissatisfied with him gives Anthony an excuse for pulling away. He's always stalking out, slamming doors, clamming up. Such withdrawal becomes his self-protective shell. Feeling vulnerable and raw, he is always pulling away from being too intimate, from caring too much.

The real source of trouble for Cindy and Anthony isn't that Cindy is a good person and Anthony a bad one. (In fact, were Cindy to divorce Anthony, she would probably marry another man just like him.) The true conflict is between their unconscious needs. Unrecognized and unresolved, these needs are the source of frustration; these needs create the gap between what Cindy and Anthony want from their marriage and what they feel they are getting. If this gap is not closed—by their uncovering the needs that give the pattern its driving force—the conflict will spin on and on. As Cindy and Anthony begin to understand their needs, they can start to make their different natures work to support each other instead of to tear each other apart.

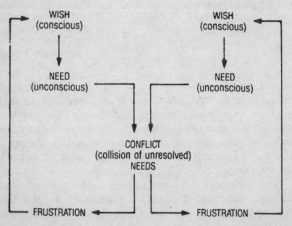

IS THIS YOUR PATTERN OF CONFLICT?

You may be wondering how Cindy and Anthony's conflict and needs apply to you. Perhaps you do have a need like Cindy's to deny your anger. Perhaps your husband, like Anthony, is trying to protect himself. But you and your man are different—or at least it seems so: the events and circumstances of your lives don't match theirs. How then are you to know if your needs are like theirs? We'll show you how we uncovered their needs and how you can uncover yours.

Needs are revealed in the complaints we have about each other. If you pay careful attention to the gripes and criticism that are hurled about, you can root out your needs.

Undoubtedly that sounds surprising. Surprising but true. Each complaint is a clue about the impact you have on your partner (or he on you).

Suppose you've complained as Cindy has about Anthony: "He clams up, or walks out on me when he's angry." What can this tell you?

These are actions that isolate. If you think about it, these are the ways a man can withdraw. Analyzing your complaint enables you to zero in on Anthony's need: to protect himself.

Now let's consider a complaint a man like Anthony has about Cindy (or someone like her): "When I tell somebody off she cringes and then gets terribly upset."

Can you learn about her need from this? The complaint reveals that anger is an intolerable feeling to a woman like Cindy. Its expression—even in a partner—is distressing. Her need begins to unfold: she may be in conflict over revealing a certain emotion—anger.

Obviously analyzing one complaint doesn't pinpoint a need exactly. What follows then (and what will follow in each story of Marital Gridlock) are a series of the couple's dissatisfactions and what they truly reveal. If you and your husband are like Cindy and Anthony, these complaints will ring true—you will hear an echo of the kinds of things you've been complaining about, perhaps for years.

IS YOUR HUSBAND LIKE ANTHONY?

If you think your only problem is that you are married to a "difficult" man, your husband, like Anthony, may be behaving in ways intended to keep you and everyone else from getting close. That's what analyzing your complaints will help you reveal.

Your complaint:
   "He puts people off."
Your husband's need:
   Because closeness leaves him feeling vulnerable to greater hurt he acts in ways that will keep people from coming close. He hopes, "If they don't like me, they can't get close enough to affect me."

Your complaint:
   "Whenever he doesn't like something I've done, he threatens separation or divorce. He's always telling me to get off his back or he'll walk out on me."
Your husband's need:
   If he pulls away or runs when he's upset, he's showing that the only way he knows of dealing with vulnerability is withdrawal.

Your complaint:
   "His version of an argument is to stop talking for three days. He never wants to talk about feelings."
Your husband's need:
   He may not be able to. A person can talk about feelings only when he's somewhat in control of them. Denying his feeings is his way of shielding himself from the pain they can cause him.

Your complaint:
   "He gets into sex, but when he's through he's through. We fuck but we don't make love."
Your husband's need:
   Sexual intimacy may make him feel dependent. Reducing sex to a physical rather than emotional union means his body—but not his soul—enters a woman.

Cindy complains that Anthony neglects her in certain ways. "Give Anthony free time and it's his boat, or tennis lessons, or *Sports Illustrated*. He has time for me only if I take a fit." Perhaps your husband also throws himself into solitary pursuits and hobbies in order to withdraw from intimacy, in order to shut you out.

Emotional insulation can take other forms. Many, many men use work to keep themselves out of emotional touch. Long hours may keep your man physically out of reach. Once home with his head filled with business problems, he has little energy for you and no time for closeness.

Do you find that things get their worst in social situations? Does your husband take over the conversation? Talking isn't necessarily an exchange between two people. A stream of opinions, or banter, can be as much of a barrier as is silence. Perhaps you resent that your husband is always saying that he hates your friends, your family, your co-workers. "You name it, he can't stand it." Hate is a wall he erects between himself and other people.

You may find it ironic that your man, like Anthony, seems so tough—but isn't. Yet once you develop perspective on his need to protect himself from his pain, you'll understand his behavior. Because your man feels defenseless, he may fear letting down his guard. Your husband may feel his survival depends upon encasing his vulnerability in a spiny shell that keeps you out.

ARE YOU LIKE CINDY?

Could you, like Cindy, be trying to deny your anger? Could you be struggling to avoid or reject unacceptable feelings? To answer this question is challenging. After all, how do you begin to detect angry feelings in yourself if you're doing everything to keep them at bay? That's why outside assistance can be so useful. Reviewing your partner's complaints about you can make the discovery possible. You will be able to grasp the impact you have on him.

Your husband's complaint:

"She knows I don't get along with her parents but she insists we spend time with them."

Your need:

Since you find it impossible to express your own negative or antagonistic feelings toward your parents, you need your partner to speak them for you. Every time your partner gets into a fight with them, *you* don't have to. No wonder you need him along.

Your husband's complaint:

"In bed, anything besides the missionary position makes me seem animalistic. She holds back."

Your need:

Your husband doesn't suppress his sexual appetites the way you need to. This both attracts and disturbs you. You are afraid that if you let loose in bed, you may let loose outside your bedroom.

Your husband's complaint:

"She knew I was no angel when she married me. This is the way I am. Period."

Your need:

A "difficult" man is your insurance policy. As long as he remains the devil, you can feel angelic by comparison.

Your husband's complaint:

"I always feel her eyes following me, watching to see what I'm going to mess up. It's like she's in a lifeguard's chair supervising from above, telling me how to behave."

Your need:

This is part of your struggle to eliminate anything you perceive as negative. You feel that you have to be nice all the time—and you want your marriage, your home, your life to be nice too. This involves watching, correcting, and supervising your husband —the one who brings disorder and anger into your life.

Your husband's complaint:

"I feel lousy that I'm making her miserable. Maybe I'm just not good enough for her."

Your need:
> Your husband takes on the role of "baddie." After a
> while, he, too, may believe that he's "bad." Your
> need is forcing you and your husband into good guy/
> bad guy roles.

You may notice something about Anthony's complaints.
By and large, Anthony doesn't have bad things to say
about Cindy—in fact, quite often he puts himself down.
This imbalance is revealing. If in a relationship, one
partner seems to be the "bum," the "louse," the "bad guy,"
he may be carrying the load of angry feelings you avoid
calling your own. If you believe your marriage would be
fine if only your husband were nicer, more refined, friend-
lier, kinder—look again. Your struggle to make your
partner nice, to throw out the negatives, may be the very
struggle you wage within yourself.

This idea about anger may be confusing. After all,
Cindy does get angry—at Anthony. But the point is that
she feels provoked into being irritated and annoyed. You
too may feel that you're not an angry person, that "the
devil made you do it." You are a good-natured person
made angry by a bad husband. This secondhand anger is
the only sort you feel free to express. Wishing to hold on to
a view of yourself as "good," you connect with a man who
can take the fall for you.

WHERE DOES YOUR NEED COME FROM?

You can guess by the way a need affects you, by the
force it exerts on your relationships, that it does not spring
up overnight. Your need has a history: its sources lie in
your past. It developed from your earliest relationship with
your family, your parents and siblings. *Your need is the
unfinished business of your childhood.* It intrudes on your
adult relationships, coloring your perceptions of those you
love. As long as you carry around this emotional baggage,
you will repeat your conflicts. (How many times have you
said about friends, "She divorced one bum only to marry
another just like him.") Without being aware of it, your

need colors the way you view your world. Unconsciously, you interpret much of what your partner says or does in light of your need, your early experience.

Since your need derives from your past, the way to learn about it is to examine your childhood. In the next sections, we will look at Anthony's and Cindy's early years and—if you and your husband are like them—at what your pasts must have been like. Though superficial aspects may be different, look to see if the essences of their childhoods resemble yours and your husband's. People like Cindy and Anthony flounder because they are caught acting out with each other the old, unfulfilled scenarios of childhood. Connect your needs with your emotional histories and relax the grip your past has on you.

ANTHONY'S PAST

"In the car, I listen to this radio psychologist, Dr. Goldstein. The other day she discussed agoraphobia—it happens mostly to women. They don't leave their houses because they panic if they do. I don't think my mother was like that; she never got an attack, but I always remember her being at home. Maybe you could get her to go to the beauty parlor once in a while. Lots of times, she stayed in her housedress all day. Her friends would come in for coffee or she would talk on the telephone. The telephone was a big thing. You'd think with all that time at home she'd be a great housekeeper or a wonderful cook. She wasn't. She always seemed to be nervous, worried about my two brothers and my father. Even at home she'd keep tabs on us. You couldn't close a door for long before you'd hear, 'What's going on in there?' She'd even walk in on me or my brothers in the bathroom. If she didn't hear you, she was worried you'd gotten hurt in the tub. It could bug you as a kid but as I got older I didn't take her so seriously."

Anthony's adolescence was tumultuous. "I was wild. I was in Catholic school where they loved rules. I broke every one they ever invented. I don't know how I stayed in—except that my mother was always on the phone asking that I be given 'just one more chance.'" Anthony's father's reaction was different. "Dad would be upset but he'd always tell me, 'Don't worry about what your mother says: I know deep down you're a good boy.'"

Anthony's father was less of a presence in the house. "Most nights my dad came home after we had dinner. Sunday was his only day off. He was an old-fashioned, hardworking guy. He spent a lot of energy on his dry cleaning business—though he never missed Thursday night poker with the boys. By the time I was fifteen, he had four stores. He always used to tell me and my brothers, 'A man needs his own business, that way you don't answer to anyone except yourself and the big boss upstairs.' It didn't always make it easy on my mother—at home with three boys—but you gotta respect a guy like my father who's a self-made man."

Anthony claims that he learned not to take his mother so seriously, but actually she affected him greatly. Since she filled up her empty life with nervous worry about her family, she was unable to be an interested, concerned mother and instead was prying and meddling. Because her own problems left her unable to tune into her children's true needs, she was in some fundamental way neglectful. This was especially confusing to Anthony because she was physically present all the time. She was both "on top of" Anthony and unavailable—intrusive rather than involved.

Anthony's father, in a different way, also offered his family little emotional contact and assistance; he used work as an escape. His actions conveyed the message that a man handles the emotional demands of life (and a wife) by withdrawal and isolation. Anthony's father failed the people who needed him most—his children—and in a way that was confusing to them. How could Anthony feel hurt by someone whose absence at home was a sign of fatherly devotion?

Deep inside, Anthony feels the hurt of his parents' failure to respond. It is a hurt and anger he is reluctant to acknowledge and to admit to himself. Instead, he excuses his father by "respecting him" and lets his mother off by tuning her out. Anthony is a man with two parents who feels like an orphan. As a child he learned to protect himself from his pain by remaining aloof, and even today he keeps up this defensive strategy.

IS THIS YOUR HUSBAND'S PAST?

Could your man, the one who makes life seem so rough, really be a hurt and vulnerable little boy adept at keeping you, or for that matter everyone, from getting close?

Reading about Anthony's past may already have you saying, "That's it—that's my man." But in case you're not certain, here are some clues that will help you make connections. You see, certain aspects of childhood are common to all people with this need. We've isolated some of the most important elements, the benchmarks, of this need in the making. If your man is like Anthony, you are about to learn a lot about his innermost feelings.

He was a hell-raiser, a troublemaker, a difficult kid— especially as a teenager.

When a parent doesn't respond positively, a child is left feeling angry. He discovers that the only way to get attention is by provoking a negative reaction. As an adult, he may continue to be provocative because that is the only way he knows to connect.

His teenage vocabulary consisted of, "Stop bugging me," "Buzz off," and "Get off my back."

As a child he coped the only way he could—by angrily pushing away, closing himself off. As a man, he may be unable to stop pushing.

His mother insisted on knowing what was going on. She was pushy and prying.

Every child needs privacy. A boy with an intrusive mother can become a man who feels all women will eat him up alive. Maybe that's why he angrily insists on keeping his distance.

His mother spent a lot of time at home but she wasn't a good mother.

Simply being physically present doesn't mean a par-

ent is there emotionally. This is confusing. It leaves a man unable to pinpoint his hurt. Instead he just pulls away.

His father was a busy man, a hard worker. He tried to create a better life for his children.

A father like this leaves little time for his family. His children may feel grateful for the effort but hurt, sad, and even angry over lost opportunities.

The roots of Anthony's need lie in a father who wasn't around very much and a mother who never gave him a moment's peace. Was lack of involvement from one parent and over-involvement from another a central theme of your man's childhood too?

Does your man have a mother who was on his back? Perhaps that's why he grew into a man who's on *your* mother's back—a sort of reversing of the roles.

If any of this rings true, remember: a man who acts as if he is angry at the whole world is likely to have been a child whose world was full of hurt.

Now take a glimpse at Cindy's past. Could it be yours?

CINDY'S PAST

Ask Cindy about her childhood and she'll pour forth vivid memories—but mainly of her younger brother, Larry. "He was a problem for my parents from day one. I can't remember his colic stage or his 'getting into everything' stage (although I do recall his trip to the emergency room for the aspirin he ate), but I can certainly remember his temper tantrums. My parents tried so hard with him. They're such gentle, refined people. My brother was anything but. He could exhaust my mother. When I came home from school and heard, 'Go up to your room and be a good girl,' I knew Larry had given her a rough time."

Cindy felt sorry for her parents and her brother. Even as an adult, she gets distraught and tearful thinking about him. "He had so many opportunities, but he just couldn't make it. He works for the railroad. All his friends and cousins are college graduates—I think he feels he is a failure. He doesn't even come home for Christmas."

Cindy, on the other hand, was the light of her parents' life—and still is. Affectionate, pretty, and a good student, Cindy always impressed adults, whether it was the teacher who found her "a pleasure in class," or the dinner guest who would invariably remark about "the lovely young lady." "I was no angel, but I liked being helpful. I was even-tempered. In fact, my mother told me that she never needed to take my temperature. If I got cranky, or didn't act like myself, it was a sure sign I had a fever.

"I basically did not give my parents grief. The only thing that came close was when I broke my engagement with Brad. On paper, Brad had it all. We're from the same hometown and church. He's Ivy League, a football player, good-looking. But he was just too regular. I remember one weekend we had my parents' house to ourselves. Our wedding was a month off. We were on my parents' bed into heavy petting and we got excited and took off our clothes to have sex. Suddenly, Brad stopped dead. He lost his erection. He got terribly serious, looked at me, and said, 'Cindy, we can't do this to our parents.' I couldn't believe it—I thought he was a man. I figured if he couldn't be one before the wedding, he'd never be one after. I saw myself the way I'd be for the rest of my life—in a big house in the suburbs meeting the girls for lunch. No way I was settling for that. My parents were mortified, but I wouldn't change my mind. One thing you can't say about Anthony is that he's boring.

"Still, I know my parents will stop complaining about Anthony when we give them grandchildren—I know how much they'll enjoy that."

For Cindy, little has changed since childhood. Providing pleasure has always been the role conferred on her. Being a pleasant girl has had its rewards: attention, love, closeness with her parents. But it also has limitations. There was an unspoken agreement that Cindy would not get mean, angry, unpleasant. It was as if family love and acceptance was conditional on her maintaining a positive role.

Openly expressed anger was absent in Cindy's life. In-

stead there was a decided emphasis on refinement, gentil-
ity, courtesy at all times. To a child like Cindy, unpleasant
feelings were ugly, perhaps even dangerous, something
prohibited, to be suppressed. Cindy's relationship with her
brother, Larry, underscored all this. For any child, the arrival of a younger sibling stirs emotions, from excitement
and delight to jealousy and irritation. From time to time,
every child feels angry, not only toward his or her siblings
but also toward his or her parents, whose loyalty, time, and
energy are now divided. But if you have a "troubled"
brother, expressing those natural feelings makes you feel
like you're kicking someone who's already on the ground.
And becoming irritated with parents who send the silent
but powerful message, "Things are so bad with him, you
can't let us down," is also impossible.

For Cindy, one demand came on many fronts: bury your
"ugly" feelings, don't let them show. She didn't, at least
not directly. Instead, she found a man through whom those
pent-up feelings could be expressed.

IS THIS YOUR PAST?

Do you, like Cindy, avoid acknowledging and expressing the anger you feel? If the kind of childhood we are
about to describe sounds like yours, you'll begin to understand how you developed this need and how it affects your
life as an adult.

Your parents were shy, tense, reserved, or quiet—not
the type to break up with laughter, shout, explode, let
loose in any way.
  *If your parents kept a lid on any surge of feelings,
  you may have felt that there was some danger to
  letting your emotions surface full force. As an adult,
  you tend to get tearful when you see or hear upset-
  ting things. Tears feel more comfortable than anger.*

You brought home boys your parents loved, but you
didn't stick with them. You rejected boyfriends because
they were so dull, unexciting, too sweet.
  With your need, nice guys do finish last. You needed

"an angry young man" to express your unacceptable feelings.

You have a sibling who doesn't seem to belong, who is troubled, difficult, an outcast.
This may have left you feeling that your family rejects anyone who doesn't quite fit. And knowing that your sibling was the bad guy while you were supposed to be the good guy, you may have forced your natural feelings of jealousy and anger underground.

Think about the way your parents treated you.

Did they spout the sort of comments Cindy used to hear? "Whenever she's hungry she gets out of sorts," "If she's grumpy she must be coming down with something," "She never misbehaves unless she's tired," "She isn't acting like herself, she must be under the weather." Perhaps like Cindy you too had parents who couldn't tolerate or accept negative feelings unless they attributed them to causes—hunger, fatigue, illness, and so forth. They rejected the possibility that negative feelings existed as legitimate, independent feelings in you. Perhaps you still run a fever rather than let your blood boil?

You might also consider how you treated your parents. Have you rarely expressed intense feelings toward them—resentment, rage, hatred? Has the biggest problem to date been your husband? At some moments in life it's inevitable and natural to be angry—even very angry—with parents. If between the two of you, your husband is the only one who ever hated your parents, be aware that you like Cindy may have spent a childhood rejecting and denying intolerable feelings.

The kind of family Cindy had isn't the only situation that may make a child fearful of self-expression. Were you adopted or a child of divorce? Did you lose someone close at an early age? These circumstances can raise fears in a young child's imagination: fears of loss of place, status, love. An adopted child may believe unless she's "good" she'll be sent back. A child of divorce may think "bad" children, like "bad" spouses, can be divorced. A little girl's interpretation of death may be that the loved person "left" because she did something wrong. If these fears are reinforced by a parent's excessive demands that the child be good, the frightened child may try to deny and reject "badness" in herself.

Perhaps you were a girl who couldn't really be herself emotionally. You may need to have a man as your "other half"—the "bad" half you can't risk calling your own.

Anthony and Cindy are a study in contrasts. Perhaps you and your husband also come from families that are ethnically, socially, and culturally different. Why do such opposites attract—and conflict?

Your husband, a man in need of protection, unconsciously *wants* to be different from the family he marries into. It's his best defense against closeness. He can then stand apart rather than be a part of your family. For you, with a need to deny aspects of yourself, in-laws who are looser, louder, sloppier than you are express the side of your personality you try to control.

Happily, once conflicting needs are resolved—as they will be in the final chapter—opposites can attract for all the right reasons.

Now that you've met Cindy and Anthony and learned about their pattern of conflict, their needs, their complaints, and their pasts, did anything sound familiar? Is there any similarity between Anthony and Cindy's marriage and your own? Perhaps something quite specific fell into place. Perhaps not. After all, this is only the first of eight accounts of Marital Gridlock—it can't be everybody's story. Or perhaps you are still unsure about how to recognize your pattern in the description of another couple's lives. In the next chapter, before we go on to the other couples in gridlock, we help you examine certain aspects of your life and your past. This will sharpen your skills of self-observation, so that you can uncover your own pattern of conflict. Keep that goal in sight—the reward is a marriage filled with satisfaction and love.

Just bear in mind one additional thought. Many women are startled by just how closely a couple in these pages captures their marital problem. It's as if a light of recognition suddenly flashes on. But we don't expect that precise and startling fit to always occur. If it happens—excellent; it may be enlightening, even exhilarating. But in all likelihood insight may come more gradually. As you read, listen to the voices of self-awareness stir within you. Somewhere, if you are willing to listen you may not be startled into self-knowledge, but its light may slowly start to shine.

Uncovering Your Own Pattern

❧ ❦

In "Beauty and the Beast" we have been looking beneath the surface in order to understand a couple's interaction. You too are capable of observing a couple, reflecting on their actions, and perhaps speculating on the meaning of their behavior. You've probably done it many times without realizing it; you've come home from many parties, for example, and discussed some of the couples with whom you shared the evening, trying to figure out "What's really going on between them." You might have said, for instance, "Bill and Leslie can't talk without disagreeing—they're so competitive." Or, "Joan and Roger are like night and day. She's so quiet. I think she has a lot to offer but Roger comes on so strong, he could intimidate anyone. What an ego!" Without much effort, you've analyzed behavior.

It isn't as simple to observe yourself. When you're emotionally involved, you lose your objectivity. You are missing an essential ingredient—distance. Now, we will begin to help you gain the insight acquired from stepping back and observing your own relationship. As you read about the couples in Marital Gridlock, you will discover how to use your ability to analyze others and their needs as a springboard to understanding yourself. As you learn to recognize the key elements in the patterns of couples like Anthony and Cindy, you can begin to make comparisons with your own situation. Since the lives of these couples reflect the most common conflict patterns, you may well find similarities with your own situation. But even if your pattern fails to leap out from the page at you, reading about each relationship gives you a chance to reflect on your own, a chance to gain distance.

UNDERSTANDING YOUR HIDDEN NEEDS

What exactly should you look for to uncover your needs? As we saw with Cindy and Anthony, your complaints about each other can help reveal your needs. Start by trying to identify the central theme running through your dissatisfaction. Each of your arguments, hurts, and disappointments may appear different—but each is actually a facet of a core conflict. What is the unifying force, the common denominator, behind your criticism, your unhappiness, your concerns?

Think of Cindy and the complaints Anthony has: that she forces him to spend time with her family, that she is the nice girl in bed, that she's always on his back, that she's too good for him. The common theme is that Cindy has to be nice, to be the good guy, wanting Anthony to express her anger for her. And Anthony? Cindy complains that he withdraws from her, that he puts people off, that he doesn't have time for her. Anthony is protecting himself; he just can't be close to Cindy.

Now try to find the themes in your conflict. Spend some time considering your concerns and complaints. Would you or your husband say:

"Our house is a pigsty."
"He can't hold a job."
"I can't do anything right."
"He doesn't let me meet his kids."
"Everyone's more important than I am."
"He lets the kids get away with murder."
"She only knows how to spend money."
"We haven't had sex in a month."
"He won't give up his apartment."

"All she does is yell."
"She's an impossible flirt."
"We both need a wife."
"Her checkbook's a disaster area."
"She's never off the phone."
"He's screwing around."
"All he does is work."
"He doesn't lift a finger at home."
"He's asleep in front of the TV every night."
"He forgets my birthday and our anniversary."
"His ex-wife won't leave us alone."
"He always wants me to pay my own way."
"He's always so pushy."
"She always has to be right."
"Why doesn't she need a career at this stage?"

Do any other complaints come to mind? Give yourself time to consider any dissatisfactions you may have. Write them down. Hold on to this list as you move on to the other couples—it will prove useful.

Once you've noted your complaints, look beyond the surface gripes. Review them, asking yourself, "What are the underlying issues?" (You might try pretending that a friend has shared this private information with you and wants your perspective on her marriage. This will help you be more objective.) Could any of the following lie at the heart of your difficulties? Check those that may apply.

Jealousy	Disappointment
Competitiveness	Suspiciousness
Control	Respect
Domination	Perfection
Mothering (Smothering)	Self-esteem
Reliability	Communication
Sharing	Fear
Negligence	Mutuality
Trust	Abandonment
Dependency	Aggression
Unavailability	Ego
Intrusiveness	Passivity
Abuse	Withdrawal
Hurt	

Try to connect your complaints to the basic emotions they reflect. Then as you read the Complaint/Need sections of each couple, you will be better able to compare them to your own. Gaining insight into your dissatisfaction will help you and your husband understand each other. Being able to make connections between complaints and needs allows you to achieve a change of perspective. In the final chapter we will show you how to use your changed perspective to improve your marriage. Instead of accusing each other, you and your husband will be able to communicate.

RELEASING THE HOLD OF YOUR PAST

As we saw in Anthony's and Cindy's lives, your needs are the unfinished business from your childhood. As you begin to understand how the past affects the present, you can begin to loosen its hold. You will need to discover how your childhood gave rise to your needs. Begin making connections between past and present. Think back. Recall. Here are some considerations that may be helpful:

What is your earliest memory of your mother, father, brothers, and sisters?

What was your attitude toward them? Theirs toward you? Toward one another?

How did your relationships with your siblings affect your development?

Who were the people most important to you in your early life?

Were there any other significant people in your childhood? Grandparents? Aunts? Uncles? Teachers? Neighbors? Friends?

How did they contribute to your personality?

What is/was your parents' marriage like? What sort of people are/were they together and apart from each other?

What was the style of your family? Was it, for example, close-knit or distant, competitive or supportive, relaxed or tense, autocratic or democratic, angry or happy, direct or indirect, and so forth?

What was the emotional atmosphere? Did any feelings predominate? Were any absent?

Did you have a good childhood? How did your parents treat you?

What do you know or remember about your childhood milestones—walking, talking, first day of school, first menstrual period, first date, etc.?

What was your school and social life like?

How was your adolescence?

Were there any extreme or unusual circumstances—for example, illness, emotional problems, alcohol, drugs, gambling, abuse, divorce, adoption, separations, infidelity, molestation, death—in your childhood?

What are your sexual memories? What were your family's and your own sexual attitudes and values?

These questions will give rise to others of your own. Let that happen. The more you inquire, the more you uncover. As you start to flesh out the picture, you will get an indication of the way your past affected the kind of person you are today. Don't expect everything to become immediately apparent. These connections between the child and adult in you are complicated and subtle. That's where the eight couples come in handy. As you read about their pasts, you will discover one remarkably like your own. This will help you gain insight into how your past created your need, the need that plays such a central role in your relationship with your partner.

You will find it a great relief to gain insight into the pattern of your conflict. When you unearth your pattern, you clarify your behavior. Your actions and emotions become comprehensible to you and to those you love. As soon as you can say, "So that's why I feel this way," "So this is why I do this," "So that's why I say that," you make an important emotional shift. In such self-awareness lies the potential for change, the potential for taking charge of your relationships.

You see, your response to your unconscious needs has become habitual—an emotional habit that controls you. But once you add awareness, you also add an important step between your impulses and your actions—thought. You will become self-reflective, able to say, "Here I go again." This won't necessarily safeguard you from repeating your conflicts. But it gives you a moment in which to say no to yourself, to your needs. You gain freedom. And with free choice, you can say no to conflict, yes to a more gratifying relationship.

For some people all it takes is insight to break out of a pattern. But there is more to be done. Much more. There are numerous ways to apply newly gained understanding to your everyday life together. In fact, once you've had an opportunity to discover which of the eight patterns is yours, you will be ready to put into action the techniques we have designed to help you renew your marital bonds.

Now on to Sarah and Chris. Perhaps you and your husband also march to the beat of a different drummer.

SARAH and CHRIS:
To the Beat of a
Different Drummer

୬ ୧

Chris's damp shirt clung to his body. The bus terminal's air-conditioning proved ineffective against August's stifling heat. Chris wished himself back on the porch of his in-laws' summer cottage. Meeting his wife, Sarah, due on the 4 P.M. bus from Charlottesville, had required this departure from more pleasant surroundings. Fortunately Chris had decided to leave their two children playing on the beach with Grandma and Grandpa. Sarah would be disappointed, but with the bus an hour late she'd appreciate his decision. Chris felt himself getting irritated. Why should he worry about Sarah's disappointment? Those were the sacrifices she had to make—her new promotion to hospital administrator had prompted her decision to pass up the three-week vacation and instead make the weekend trips from home. The thought that work had become such a priority for Sarah sparked ambivalent feelings in Chris. Though he hadn't been the one tied down to the kids and house for fifteen years, Chris felt he understood—at least intellectually—the drawbacks: the boredom and frustration that set in, the self-doubt and social pressure that had made Sarah reply, "Just a housewife," to endless cocktail party queries. But he also knew work was no paradise. Did Sarah realize how good she had had it all the years he was working his tail off? Wasn't her second shot at things a luxury Chris had made possible? A luxury that was now, ironically, depriving him of his wife. Chris found himself edging toward resentment. Recalling past summers made it more aggravating. True, years had gone by when family vacations weren't possible: as a young internist starting out in private practice he had worked seven days a week, twelve months a year. It had been this drain on his time that had pushed him toward the group practice he currently shared; it had made the last seven summers at the beach possible. Now even those were fast becoming a memory.

Chris was stirred from his daydream by Sarah's voice shouting a greeting from the bus as it rolled in. Dressed in a suit—she had come directly from the office—she looked like the ultimate professional. Yet he knew her well enough—in an hour, surrounded by the family, she would look as if her life was devoted to being a wife and mother. Resentment softened into admiration. When he kissed her, the rough edges of his feelings smoothed out. Despite the complications, this was a woman he loved deeply.

In his arms, Sarah, apologizing up and down for the inconvenience caused by the delay, felt only Chris's love. Once settled into the cool, comfortable drive she erupted with news of her week. The job promotion was novel enough to create the excitement she had longed to share with Chris all week; and the wage increase had come through—another 10 percent jump in her already substantial salary. Sarah didn't fool herself; salary was a big part of her decision to climb the career ladder. She could remember the dress purchased with her first paycheck. Chris had never attached strings to money; still, the notion of *her own* money made a difference.

Fifteen minutes into her excited banter, Sarah began to realize her enthusiasm wasn't shared. She asked, "What's wrong, Chris?" His reply stung. "Isn't it enough that you're at work all week, are you going to carry on about it all weekend too?" A lump throbbed in Sarah's throat; the hot tears that smarted in her eyes were as much from pain as from anger—it was all right for him to go on about his patients but she wasn't allowed to go on about her job. Or was she—provided she had been around to do the laundry first? Despite these thoughts, Sarah opted for silence, determined not to enter her parents' house in the middle of an argument.

It didn't help. After hugs and kisses for all, her mother with her usual alertness picked up on the tension. Leaving the crew downstairs, she took Sarah upstairs to "unpack." Once the door closed, her mother made her opinions known. "I'm going to be blunt. Chris hasn't hidden his feelings from us—he misses you and he's not happy about the way things are." Her mother didn't stop for breath. "It's very good to have a job—even at my age I envy you—but a full-fledged career when you have a family counting on you, that's something else. You may be my own daughter, but I'm warning you—don't get pigheaded and end up sorry. And while Chris isn't the envious sort, becoming an administrator at his hospital with all those doctors streaming in and out of your office is playing with fire."

This was too much. A lecture when what she needed was help. Sarah stormed out of the room and headed for the beach. The next speech would be "Look how satisfied your sister Frieda is with her volunteer work." Sarah was fuming, only the thought of a long swim by herself kept her from exploding.

No sooner was she out of the water than her boys, Aaron and Daniel, were right beside her jabbering away about soccer games, swimming lessons, and the high dive that ten-year-old Aaron had finally managed to take. "Remember my first try? Aaron was a pro by comparison. I wish you could have seen him, Mom," fifteen-year-old Daniel lamented. Sarah, staring across the water, wondering why she couldn't be a more successful juggler of her life, wished the same.

Evening brought a respite from tensions. Her father barbecued ribs—their favorite—and her mother, despite impossible summer heat, made a sweet potato pie that heartily contributed toward making everyone around the dinner table content and lighthearted. They could even laugh when Aaron piped up, "Grandma, would you come to live with us? I think Mommy and Daddy need a wife like you."

Later that night the relaxed feelings carried over into sex as Sarah and Chris made love on the beach. Both of them began to apologize and promises not to be so sensitive were exchanged.

The three days flew by reminiscent of former summers. Sarah even managed to make a rhubarb pie, as if she had never stopped being a full-time mother. On Monday afternoon the reality of Sarah's leaving became painful. The boys started being whiny, and Chris snapped about having to break up a beautiful day just to make a bus. And only Sarah's scowls kept her parents' comments in check.

The car ride to the terminal was nearly as silent as the one in from it had been. In the quiet, Sarah wondered if she was doing the right thing and Chris once more found himself torn—Sarah was seeming more like a roommate these days than a wife. The bus was being boarded as they pulled in. A quick kiss, hurried good-byes, and Sarah was off.

While he watched the bus depart Chris's resentment grew. It was the same feeling he had had the week earlier, and on that Monday evening, not wanting to be alone, he had headed for Irene's Place, a singles club. Within a few hours Chris was in bed with Jackie, a secretary on a week-long vacation.

Angry at Sarah, he couldn't have cared less about fidelity. As far as Chris was concerned it was Sarah who had pushed him into it. Only because of all the recent publicity about herpes had they not had intercourse. But when he had seen Sarah this weekend, his true feelings finally caught up with him. It wasn't the fear of herpes that had stood in his way. He cared for Sarah. Screwing around with other women wasn't his interest and wouldn't solve their problems. Now standing alone in the terminal he regretted Sarah's quick departure. There hadn't been enough time. For another week the rough edges of their mutual hurt would go untouched.

DISCERNING THE PATTERN OF CONFLICT

Unlike many couples in a crisis, Sarah and Chris essentially share the same wish: both want to cope successfully with the changing nature of their contemporary lifestyle. Sarah candidly admits, "I guess my real wish is to make everybody happy—including myself." And Chris is aware that in all fairness he's got to make adjustments: "What I want is to be able to cope with all these changes, not just survive them. I'm trying to be the 'new man.'" Yet they feel overwhelmed by the magnitude of this adjustment, and despite good intentions dissension erupts.

Is Sarah's job the problem? Only on the surface. What is the true source of their conflict? While their wishes may be parallel, their needs are not. Sarah has an unconscious need to establish her own identity—something that was not an emotional priority at the time she married. Her interest in moving beyond her home cannot be reduced to the stereotype of the bored housewife looking for change. Rather, she is, as an adult, experiencing a kind of delayed identity crisis, one facilitated by the changing social climate.

By contrast, Chris, despite all his intellectual understanding of the "new woman," has an unconscious need to keep the status quo, to hold on to the old models and maintain the old roles—breadwinner, husband, boss, and so forth.

It is Sarah's compelling need to break with convention and Chris's need to hang on to it that is the source of their conflict. These unconscious forces create frustration: Sarah feels she gets insufficient support, and Chris feels he suffers too many demands. They are two people who started out playing by the same set of rules only to find a new set instituted midstream. The tension of their mutual frustration is mitigated by their deep attachment. Yet each of them is beginning to feel estranged from the other and unsure of how to bridge the widening gap of discontent.

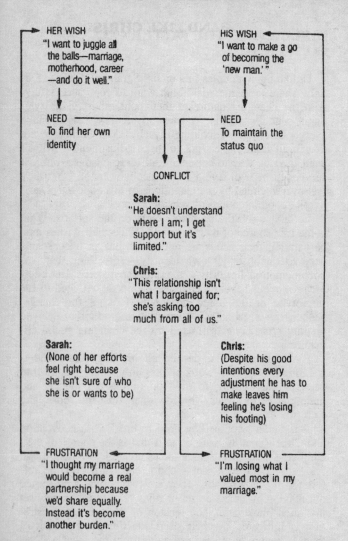

HER WISH
"I want to juggle all
the balls—marriage,
motherhood, career
—and do it well."

HIS WISH
"I want to make a go
of becoming the
'new man.'"

NEED
To find her own
identity

NEED
To maintain the
status quo

CONFLICT

Sarah:
"He doesn't understand
where I am; I get
support but it's
limited."

Chris:
"This relationship isn't
what I bargained for;
she's asking too
much from all of us."

Sarah:
(None of her efforts
feel right because
she isn't sure of who
she is or wants to be)

Chris:
(Despite his good
intentions every
adjustment he has to
make leaves him
feeling he's losing
his footing)

FRUSTRATION
"I thought my marriage
would become a real
partnership because
we'd share equally.
Instead it's become
another burden."

FRUSTRATION
"I'm losing what I
valued most in my
marriage."

IS YOUR HUSBAND LIKE CHRIS?

Could the crux of your conflict center on your quest for change and your husband's unconscious resistance to it? Are you, like Chris and Sarah, in an old marriage with new rules? Could your husband be afraid of change while you may be trying to break away? Don't be deceived by the superficial problems in your relationship—look for the real issues behind your complaints about each other. Some of the typical grievances of women in this situation follow, with explanations of the husband's underlying need that creates these grievances. If you and your husband are in conflict like Chris and Sarah, many of these complaints will sound painfully familiar.

Your complaint:
  "He's never
  . . . read my poetry."
  . . . looked at my sketches."
  . . . glanced at my thesis."
Your husband's need:
  His seeming disregard for your special, perhaps new, interests may really be an effort to avoid confronting changes that are brewing.

Your complaint:
  "According to him I ought to be a volunteer or work part-time."
  "He'd like my work to be a hobby."
Your husband's need:
  A part-time job would ensure a full-time companion; your man fears change will rob him of this.

Your complaint:
  "I don't want to hear how the wife of his friend at work got her Ph.D. and divorce at the same time."
  "He's always got a snide comment about a woman who's a boss, that she's a dyke, or castrating, or an aggressive bitch."
Your husband's need:
  By associating a woman's accomplishments with her

failures in personal life, your husband may be revealing how threatened he feels. A put-down may be an effort on his part to stay on top.

Your complaint:

"When I'm too tired for sex, I resent being teased that he's going to have an affair with someone at work."

Your husband's need:

If he's threatening, even facetiously, he may be indicating what's really threatening him—that you'll have an affair with someone at work.

Your complaint:

"I don't think he truly respects what I'm doing. Even without meaning to, he puts me down."

Your husband's need:

Minimizing or devaluing your efforts is his way of coping with the discomfort it provokes. Unconsciously, he soothes himself by establishing that your achievements are insignificant.

Sarah complains, "Even now that I work, he'll still ask me why I've spent money on something." Perhaps your husband does the same. Money is power. Attempting to keep the status quo when financial arrangements shift may reflect his reluctance to share this power base.

Does your husband often upset you by telling you how your child hates coming home to an empty house? Your husband knows your Achilles' heel and hopes that guilt may keep you from changing in ways that frighten him.

Perhaps you feel "He wouldn't pass up a promotion in a million years, but I'm supposed to, so we can spend more time together as a family." Although your husband's interest in ensuring the quality of your family life is sincere, his concern may reflect his unconscious need not to be outdone.

Do you find yourself saying to friends, "He'll show off about 'his' wife's new job (degree, promotion, project); then to me he'll complain that there are no clean shirts." Your spouse *is* proud of you. But pride doesn't eliminate the ambivalence he feels about change.

Do you complain, "At a party, he'll always bring up the topic of my wanting to go back to work (or school) and get his friends to put it down as a bad idea." Your husband is not alone—many men are contending with the same struggle. This need is rooted in long-standing attitudes about the role of men.

ARE YOU LIKE SARAH?

Might you, like Sarah, be something of a late bloomer? Could the source of your marital conflict be, in part, a delayed identity crisis? How does your spouse characterize you? Would the following bear any similarity to his complaints?

As you review these criticisms, the latent need behind them will become clear—perhaps your need will become clear to you as well.

Your husband's complaint:
    She can get so angry, as if it's my fault she's not happy."
Your need:
    Rejecting authority is a classic feature of this need at work. When you were a girl your parents would have been the authority to oppose; now that you are a woman your husband may take on this role in your eyes.

Your husband's complaint:
    "She'll break her back to make a great dinner party, but heaven help me if I ask her to make something special."
Your need:
    Sending confusing messages may reflect your inner turmoil.

Your husband's complaint:
    "I'm accused of having exploited her."
Your need:
    Old social norms have been an obstacle to your

growth. Your spouse may represent everything that
has stood in your way till now.

Your husband's complaint:
"If I comment about her coming home late from
work, she lashes back that compared to all the men
in the office, she's the first to leave."
Your need:
The legacy of your delayed move toward independence is that you're caught with commitments in two
different worlds. This can make you feel torn.

Your husband's complaint:
"I want more children; it could hurt her career." "I
want to retire; she's looking for a promotion." "I
need her for tennis doubles; she's spending Saturday
in the library." "I'm taking the kids out for pizza
because she's at an art class." "I want to have sex;
she has to unwind."
Your need:
Your changing self-image has its impact—you and
your man now march to the beat of different drum-
mers.

Finding an identity involves rebellion. You test the
limits to extremes until you find your own pace. Meanwhile, your husband will be distressed; he will complain
that you behave differently, that you're unpredictable.

The support of a peer group is an essential element in
moving toward a personal sense of self. But your husband
may object, "Our time together is limited as it is. And still
you want a night with your girlfriends?" Your husband
says, "These days I feel more like a roommate than a husband. I used to think I was the most important thing in your
life." In trying to separate, you appear to your husband to
be withdrawing. You don't want to be alone, but to stand
on your own.

Your husband asks, "Is this the same woman I married?" No. There's the rub for him—and there's your need
at work.

Sarah and Chris are basically well-adjusted people, but
their needs keep them from readjusting as a couple. If you

and your man are caught in this conflict, you too may feel together yet far apart. You may feel as if your life is just getting off the ground, while your husband is ready for a landing.

The next question: How do two well-coordinated lives begin to pull in such separate directions? Somewhere in their pasts lies the answer.

CHRIS'S PAST

Our needs arise from early experience—which need not be synonymous with early difficulties. In Chris's case searching for trauma and pain would prove fruitless; his childhood was happy and relatively uneventful. Chris's need is a product of the time, of the attitudes that were prevalent when he was being raised.

Chris's father was a physician, who could best be described as a family doctor. "Dad's office was attached to our house. Once my two sisters and I were school age, my mother went back to being his receptionist. I think we were better known as 'Dr. Karl's kids,' than by our own names. We always knew it was a compliment. My father is probably as close to a real-life Marcus Welby as you can get." It was admiration for his father plus his family's tacit expectations that led Chris to medicine. "No one ever pressured me but I just naturally assumed, along with everyone else, that I'd be a doctor."

Much of Chris's childhood rested on a set of unspoken standards and quiet expectations. It meant, among other things, being treated differently from his sisters. "Unless my father had a house call, every night was the same. My sisters helped set the table with my mother. I'd stick with my father. In those 'good old days,'" Chris quipped sarcastically, "it never crossed anyone's mind to ask my father (or me, for that matter) to help: he carried his load—working hard all day—his evenings were for relaxing."

Almost every pursuit reflected the distinctions between boys and girls. "The closest my sisters got to a playing field were as spectators or cheerleaders. Not me, I was in everything from Scouts to Little League. School was different for me as well. It was obvious that I had to get good grades and go to college. My sisters, on the other hand, were checking out 'Modern Bride' by their senior year. Dolores, my oldest sister, was engaged to Chet at eighteen, and my parents were delighted."

A double standard was most evident around dating. "I can remember a time my father had to deliver a baby being given up for adoption. It occasioned a serious talk about men expecting wives to be virgins. I grew up believing that there were two kinds of girls—those who did and those who didn't."

Throughout his life, Chris subscribed to his family's values. "The only break came around the Vietnam War. I wasn't politically active and I personally didn't want to go. I used every ploy possible and never did get drafted. My father who had gone to war was irritated by what he considered my reneging on responsibility. He wasn't really happy that I went on to Washington, D.C. to specialize in neurosurgery either. It meant I wouldn't be joining him in his practice."

One Christmas when he was home on leave from his residency, Chris's mother expressed her feelings about his recent choice. "The way you've been raised I'm surprised you'd feel happy with what you're choosing. I'd think you'd want to be the kind of doctor and man your father's been." It was, in fact, just this sense that brought Chris back to Charlottesville and to Sarah, the girl he had dated casually at the University of Virginia.

How did this past fuel his need? While Chris is no carbon copy of his father, he very much identified with him. Chris is a man who has internalized the values and standards of his family and culture. Central to those is the special investment of being "the man in the family." Giving up this masculine image threatens his very comfortable sense of who he is.

IS THIS YOUR HUSBAND'S PAST?

Could your husband be burdened by this sort of past? Could he be trapped in a deeply ingrained role but threatened by its erosion? Many elements in your spouse's upbringing may give rise to a need to keep things as they are:

School was important for him. He had to think of the future. He was groomed to take on the outside world.
As with many men, this may have left him no time to know his inner world. Resistance to change can arise from his feeling ill-equipped to contend with the emotions that invariably erupt in the face of change.

The only time a girl asked him out instead of vice versa was "Sadie Hawkins Day." When in a car with a girl, he drove.
If a boy learns he's in the driver's seat, it may be a position he can't easily let go of as a man.

His mother was a full-time housewife. He enjoyed—and expected—finding her at home after school. His best moments were shared with his mother: her reading to him in bed, nursing his colds, and so forth.
Most boys derive comfort from a mother. Throughout life a woman has always been your man's support system. Losing that may be his unconscious fear. Anything less than the full-time attention of a woman makes your husband feel as if you're withdrawing your love.

In Chris's home, housework was "for girls." If your husband was taught, like Chris, to believe housework is demeaning, he, too, might find helping out at home embarrassing, even emasculating. Your spouse never learned to cook, wash, vacuum, change diapers. If as a boy he was helpless on the home front, then as a man, he relies on you. Giving this up is troubling.

Your man was a Boy Scout, a leader, a team captain. These activities teach a man that being prepared is critical.

Understandably, changes that he feels unprepared for can be disquieting. Your spouse played sports, joined teams, took sides. From these activities, a boy may learn to believe life is a game. As an adult, he may not let his guard down. He sees change as defeat, loss, a sign of weakness.

Your husband was taught that girls were the weaker sex, needing a man to protect them. The lines between boys and girls were clearly drawn, especially when it came to sex. Only a boy could initiate sex. Girls "gave in." Nice girls didn't. He and his friends talked about scoring—a condom in his wallet was a status symbol. Your husband may have learned that sex, like so many other things, was to be on his own terms. Giving up his position on top (literally and figuratively) may feel like an assault on his male prowess.

A man with Chris's need to keep things from changing is to a great extent a product of his time. Perhaps your husband's past forced him into a role that limits his capacity to be flexible.

SARAH'S PAST

Is the search for yourself the course upon which you initially embarked? Sarah's past can illuminate how and why a woman may have gotten such a late start.

"My childhood was so typical that these days it would be considered unusual," Sarah says. "It was divided into two phases. During the first dolls were the most fun. In the second, boys. The chief rite of passage was getting a bra, not burning one. And the real torture came when the boys got wind of it—my back was never safe from being snapped. The only thing more embarrassing was a boy knowing you had 'your friend.' I couldn't even bear for my father or brother to know; my mother was the only one else I'd let buy my sanitary napkins. In my life I'll never forget the Sunday Ann Marie got up to take Communion and had a big red spot on her pleated skirt. To this day I still don't wear white the first days of my period."

Sarah's mother advised her on dating. "Today it's laughable but my mother actually told me to lose at bowling.

Doug, my boyfriend, wouldn't like a girl who outdid him. What's more absurd than her advice is the fact that I took it—and I was the better bowler!"

Sarah's father also gave the same sort of "advice." "If I was studying too hard he'd warn me about eye strain: 'Boys don't make passes at girls who wear glasses.'" Yet Sarah's father took pride in her achievements. "His family had quite a few talented members. When I did well in chemistry, he might tell me I took after his cousin Casper, a metallurgist who patented a process for mining zinc. At thirteen I won a local speech contest and for the first time found out about Reverend Samuel, a great-uncle who could whip up a crowd with his Sunday sermons."

While things started to change around her, Sarah's mother didn't. "I was engaged to Ray and found out he was having sex with another girl. He tried to explain that he respected me (I was still 'a technical virgin,' having done everything but) and that these other girls meant nothing. My mother told me to forgive and forget because 'that was the way men were,' and it would be so embarrassing to have to disappoint friends and family looking forward to the engagement party. If it weren't for a young woman doctor I was close to, and a borrowed copy of the *Feminine Mystique*, I don't know if I would have believed I had the right to break it off. I've always known Chris was the right man for me, but I wonder if part of the reason I married Chris before I graduated from nursing school was because I felt guilty for what I'd done."

Like many women her age, Sarah's identity was defined by the slot in life she was to fill—mother and wife. She never questioned the unwritten rules that directed the flow of her life. Only with a changing social climate was Sarah permitted to move beyond these limits. But Sarah was not simply a passive recipient of social changes. (Many women experiencing the same changes don't and won't alter their lives radically.) Sarah was ready for it. The questions, the longing, the discontent were there brewing, as was a sense of herself as capable of more. For Sarah, social forces offered support and suggested new directions.

This match between Sarah's psychological readiness and the newly emerging cultural attitudes created Sarah's need to search for a new identity.

IS THIS YOUR PAST?

Could you have been a woman, like Sarah, held back by tacit assumptions? Were you constrained by rules, norms, standards you never thought to question? If you have any qualities of the "late bloomer" the following will sound all too familiar.

Most likely, you assumed when you grew up you'd be a wife and a mother. Your "career" fantasies were those of being a ballerina, princess, nurse, or teacher.
You dreamed rather than set goals; you grew into the set role that awaited you, instead of carving one out for yourself. Only as an adult did you gain in a more "liberated" world permission to pursue a career.

You were the "good girl." You never gave your parents cause for alarm or embarrassment. Disobedience, running around, cutting classes weren't your style.
A woman in need of breaking away was often the good little girl who didn't. An adolescent struggling for self-definition breaks rules, tests limits. If you couldn't do it then, you may be trying it now.

You wanted what everyone wanted, successfully: a bra, dates, a boyfriend, a fraternity pin, an engagement ring, a June wedding, two children, a house.
Prevailing social attitudes were a powerful force. They, rather than you, determined the nature of your personal development.

Sarah's skills and talents were encouraged only to the extent that they made her more attractive or capable as a wife and mother. Your family system may have encouraged you, too, to take on the role of valuable commodity—instead of finding out who you really are.

You believed boys are stronger, more athletic, better at

math. You accepted differences and superiorities as immutable. Only later did you realize that nothing was written in stone—that you too could excel. When you went to school, girls took home-ec, boys took shop. This distinction is significant: a girl's domain was hearth and home; only boys were groomed to "take on the world."

Did you feel vaguely discontent, incomplete? As a child, you may have longed to assert yourself but were unable to identify the problem. You may have known girls who were tough, defiant, who talked about hating their parents. You may have wanted to be defiant, but you calmed down and ended up wanting to get married like everyone else. Rebellion, a revolt against authority, is often the hallmark of breaking away. If you didn't complete this self-definition during girlhood, when you are a woman, your husband may become "the oppressor" you feel you have to overturn.

By now you've probably noticed something.

Chris and Sarah's conflict has its roots in their *similar* backgrounds. So why the difference in their respective needs?

If it were to be summed up, we might say that Chris has a deep-seated fear that he has everything to lose by change, while Sarah senses she has something to gain. Fortunately, when two people begin to understand how their very similarities have begun to make them so different from each other, it's bound to make a marriage better.

HELEN and GEORGE:
Better Off Without Him

❧ ❧

"Goddamn it," Helen sputtered, as the egg rolled off the table's edge, splattering on the kitchen floor. "That's it. Next time George wants to spend Sunday fishing he can make his own lunch. What am I anyway—the maid?" The late news blared in the next room. "Turn it down," she shouted, slamming the door. "Now he's wide awake," she muttered. "It's no wonder—he slept through half the movie tonight. Typical. I finally get him out, and he manages to ruin the evening for me."

A long bath did nothing to help Helen relax. All she could think of was how little togetherness she felt in her marriage. It wasn't that she wanted so much. A walk. A dinner out once in a while where they would talk. She couldn't remember the last time they'd held hands.

Returning to the bedroom Helen was surprised to find George already there. Without a word she got under the covers. George reached his arm around her body and put his hand over her breast. Feeling her nipples becoming erect and hard, Helen caught herself giving in. "Oh no, not this time," she decided. Throwing his hand off her, she announced, "I'm tired. Maybe you caught a nap at the movie, but I didn't. Good night."

Helen's reaction came as no surprise to George. As far as he could tell, something was always eating her. "Nothing makes her happy," he mused. "I did go with her; can I help it if I was dead tired?" But it was no use explaining how he felt. Once Helen made up her mind about something, she couldn't be budged. "Have it your way, Helen," he muttered as he turned away. George was irritated with himself. "After eighteen years I should know better," he thought. "I can't win. When I want sex, she's tired; when I leave her alone, I'm a selfish bastard. I should give up; I should just stop trying. It's a wonder I don't go looking for other women."

Other women were hardly George's style. "But divorce?" he thought. "Maybe it's time we split." George was surprised how quickly the idea of divorce came to him. Eighteen years ago he didn't know one divorced person. Even ten years ago the idea was unmentionable. Now it had become more than a fleeting notion. George was grateful that he'd be gone by five the next morning. At least there would be a little good fishing and poker with the boys, he thought as he closed his eyes.

The next day, as it was growing dark, Helen heard George pull into the driveway. He walked in, a plastic bag of fish in one hand, a bakery box in the other, and offered Helen the box. "Here's the pie you wanted."

Helen raised her eyebrows and shook her head. "When did I ask for this?"

"You said your sister might stop by tonight, that . . . you needed . . ." George couldn't finish the sentence.

"I would never have asked for a pie. Me? A pie? Don't you ever listen? You know I'm trying to diet. Besides that's all Adele would need to see. I'm the one who pushed her to Weight Watchers. And now she sees how right I was."

"You're always right, Helen. That's why our daughter went all the way to Oregon for nursing school. She loved living with a mother who's always right."

Helen fumed. "You're no success story. Look at your friends. Not my kind of people at all. I wouldn't want to be seen with most of them. You're the first and only North Greenfield bowling champion with a college degree! You should be really proud."

George felt a throbbing in his temples as his blood pressure soared. "Save your speeches for work tomorrow. The phone company loves supervisors who are right about everything. Keep it up and you'll probably get a promotion."

DISCERNING THE PATTERN OF CONFLICT

For the last eight years of their eighteen-year marriage there has been continual tension between George and Helen, punctuated by angry outbursts over what seem to be minor matters. They live in a state of constant irritation. At one time, they both resigned themselves to the inevitable and considered themselves stuck for life. But now, divorce is a reality they have both contemplated. Emotionally, they've thrown their hands up in disgust at each other as if to say, "Why bother?"

Undoubtedly, this isn't what they desire from their marriage. What do they want? Helen has a clear idea. "I've always thought a marriage should be togetherness, sharing. Not just as an arrangement for convenience but something that goes both ways. I'm really romantic, I guess. I want a loving husband who'll pay attention to me."

George is reticent about his wish, almost self-effacing. "I'm really not hard to please. Maybe it sounds funny these days, but I'm the kind of guy who has to be married."

These conscious wishes are prevented from being fulfilled by the unconscious needs that each of them bring into their marriage. Helen has a compelling need not to rely on anyone—even her husband. Ironically, while she feels romantic, her need drives her to push a man away, frustrating every attempt at emotional and sexual intimacy.

George's unconscious need is to be powerless. His need is an expression of his battered self-esteem. With Helen he acts out a need to get what he expects—nothing. Their conflict is the head-on collision of these unconscious drives.

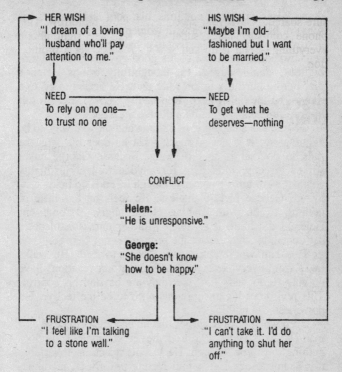

HER WISH
"I dream of a loving
husband who'll pay
attention to me."

HIS WISH
"Maybe I'm old-
fashioned but I want
to be married."

NEED
To rely on no one—
to trust no one

NEED
To get what he
deserves—nothing

CONFLICT

Helen:
"He is unresponsive."

George:
"She doesn't know
how to be happy."

FRUSTRATION
"I feel like I'm talking
to a stone wall."

FRUSTRATION
"I can't take it. I'd do
anything to shut her
off."

In every attempt George makes to connect with her, Helen focuses on the negative: what is lacking. This leaves her unable to experience any pleasure in what she is being offered and confirms her view that no one comes through for her. Thus George's pie is not a thoughtful gesture, but an obstacle to her diet. As if this isn't enough, whenever George succeeds in evoking good feelings, Helen cuts them off. Invariably the good moment becomes overshadowed by a failure, misdeed, disappointment from the past. This is at work when she counteracts her sexual excitement with the memory of George falling asleep in the movie.

And George? As a man who feels unworthy, he passively accepts Helen's criticism. He gives up easily; he withdraws. Her criticism confirms his poor self-image, his sense of being ineffective with women.

But it would be misleading to consider George the innocent bystander, for most of his good-guy gestures are ambiguous, double-edged. He thoughtfully brings Helen a pie, but he hurtfully ignores her diet. He agrees to go to a movie, but he falls asleep. Repeatedly George sets himself up for criticism by sending a double message.

George has a capacity, in a subtle and passive way, to be aggravating; it is not so much what he does but what he fails to do that is so provoking. Because George never strikes directly, it is hard for anyone to feel justifiably angry toward him. Ironically, though he ends up being criticized, George feels blameless. He feels he has little or nothing to do with making Helen angry. ("Come on, Helen, I did try.") It is Helen with her unreasonableness, her demands, who creates the problem—not George.

This behavior helps satisfy George's need. He walks away from every encounter feeling that her reactions have nothing to do with him, that they are beyond his control. This reinforces his unconscious need to be ineffective and powerless—a nothing.

Even when George senses that he becomes effective as a man (he feels Helen's arousal, her erect nipples), he does nothing to follow through. He accepts rejection. Invariably this acquiescence leaves him feeling powerless, incompetent, unable to please a woman once again.

Superficially, it is easy to see Helen and George as bad guy, good guy; shrew and henpecked husband; victimizer and victim. This is a trap of this particular pattern; it is easy to sympathize with George and miss his contribution to the problem.

This perpetual conflict leaves Helen feeling as if she can't get through to George. "It's like talking to a stone wall. With what I get from George, I might as well be alone."

George summarizes his experience, "With Helen I'm trapped. Nothing makes a dent. The only way out is to ignore her or get away." With no insight into the nature of their needs, their wishes go unmet, the conflict spins on.

Ironically, as far as their needs are concerned, George and Helen are a "perfect" match. Helen's need not to rely on anyone is confirmed by her husband—he can't do anything right therefore he can't be counted on. And George? He uses Helen to reaffirm his need. All she gives him is criticism. He ends up with what he deserves—nothing.

IS YOUR HUSBAND LIKE GEORGE?

Are you and your husband caught in a conflict like Helen and George's, where you feel dissatisfied, as if you are getting nothing, and your husband feels powerless, unable to have an impact?

Look beneath the surface of your complaints to understand your husband's need.

Your complaint:
  "He drives me crazy. He knows how to get to me."
Your husband's need:
  Passive behavior, which is typical of a man who feels powerless, often leaves you with a sense of general irritation. It's hard to pinpoint just what he does that's so provoking.

Your complaint:
  "According to him, I'm the only one who finds fault; at work everyone respects him."
  "He'll tell me that my sister (or my child or my friends) find me hard to take."
Your husband's need:
  Convincing himself that everyone has trouble with you lets him off the hook. It supports his unconscious belief that he can't make a difference.

Your complaint:
  "He's not romantic."
Your husband's need:
  Sweep a woman off her feet? Never! Your husband doesn't feel as if that power resides within him.

Your complaint:
"He doesn't see it, but he's incredibly stubborn."
"He can yes me to death—just to get me off his back."

Your husband's need:
Your husband is so convinced of his inability to have any effect on a woman that he withdraws, he stops trying.

Helen complains that George always manages to ruin things; his timing is always off. Is your husband always late? Does he always give you presents that are just a size too small? Never quite making it is a hallmark of your husband's need. This pseudoincompetence allows him to feel he can't make a woman happy. Does he always have excuses? "The boss kept me." "The car broke down." He believes that his behavior is always excusable, that outside forces prevailed. It reinforces his sense that he has no control.

Do you find that whenever you point out to your husband why you're angry, he usually responds, "It never occurred to me." Actually, what never occurs to him is the thought that he can make a difference, that he has what it takes to make you happy. You may feel that he never picks up your vibrations, that after all this time he never knows what pleases you. In fact, he blocks himself from tuning into you. This makes him unresponsive and fulfills his need to feel ineffective.

Does your husband do everything right at work, but nothing right at home? Do you feel that he's accommodating to everyone but you? By not doing anything right at home, he's demonstrating his sense that he can't make a woman happy, that he feels worthless. But by being effective at work, he shows he has the potential to get things right. Your husband is telling you that it's all there for the taking, if only you'd let him . . .

ARE YOU LIKE HELEN?

Are you, like Helen, unwilling to rely on anyone, unable to trust anyone? How does your husband describe you? Look beneath the surface of his complaints to understand your needs.

Your husband's complaint:
    "All our friends know our problems."
    "A crowded elevator is her favorite place to put me down."
Your need:
    Going public with your husband's failures is your way of convincing yourself of his lack of reliability. You try to confirm your position by getting others to agree with your view.

Your husband's complaint:
    "My friends don't like her. She's an expert at making enemies."
Your need:
    Hostility is your way of keeping people at a distance. Making the world an unfriendly place reinforces your sense that you have to go it alone.

Your husband's complaint:
    "With the whole world, I'm okay. With her, I'm a big zero."
Your need:
    This kind of discrepancy should alert you to your need. You distort your perception of your husband so that he fits your "not to be relied on" category.

Your husband's complaint:
    "I give up." "She's a shrew."
Your need:
    If you turn a man off, if he stops trying, you succeed in confirming your feelings that no one is there for you.

George complains that Helen acts so superior. Does your husband feel that he lives with an expert—in everything? Does he complain, "She's always got to be right"? Taking a position of strength, acting superior is your way of convincing yourself that you have what it takes to be independent. You have always got to be right because you don't trust anyone. Your life depends on being sure of yourself—by yourself.

Does your husband feel, "I'm damned if I do; damned if I don't"? Your need makes you unwilling to be satisfied by a man. To be satisfied means you allowed him to give; this makes you feel dependent. Perhaps he complains that the good times don't seem to last—in bed or out. You make things go sour because you are mistrustful. You fear that if things go well, it's only a matter of time till they go wrong.

Why is it that Helen and George bring these needs to their marriage? Where do these obstacles to their wishes come from?

GEORGE'S PAST

George's childhood was neither difficult nor troubled, but it can most aptly be described in the phrase, "lost in the shuffle." The third boy in the family, George at birth disappointed his parents who longed for a girl. So they decided to try again, and within a year Annie was born.

Annie, moreover, was the only granddaughter on both sides of the family. And where did this leave George? His two older brothers, close in age, had each other. With them George was always an outsider, the little boy who could never keep up. They resented his tagging along, and George would usually end up being left behind. As for his sister, she had a special position George could never have: she was the "princess" everyone had awaited.

George's mother gave him little attention. Being loved and yet ignored by his parents was confusing. Any anger and resentment he might have felt, George buried. He became, as his father would describe him, "the quiet one." "Sometimes, with George you could forget there were three boys in the house."

This forgetting seemed to occur even when George's behavior and achievement were impressive. "I don't think my mother ever really knew I made high school honor society. It went in one ear and out the other. About the only times I got rises out of my parents were when I forgot to run an errand or brought the wrong thing home from the store or messed up in some way. Those things they didn't ignore."

In high school forgetting about George became a sort of joke. "Among my friends I wasn't pushy. They'd choose a team, not giving me a position, then suddenly someone would pipe up, 'We forgot about George again,' and we'd all laugh. They were a swell bunch of guys, it didn't bother me. I never had any hard feelings about it."

With girls it was not much different. He would never tell them how he felt. "Some of the girls I really liked probably never even knew it; we'd just hang around in a group and be friendly."

Perhaps because he wasn't pushy it wasn't until he was in the Army that George had sex for the first time. "In Munich going to a whorehouse was a regular event. I just joined in with the guys. Later with Helen the difference was like night and day. I realized the sex I had been used to I just couldn't expect anymore. I didn't mind. I respected Helen. She was so full of ideas. She had enough energy for two. It was wonderful to be with someone who knew what she wanted out of life."

George's position in his family left him with a sense that he didn't make a difference. He was the outsider, always on the periphery—there was little he could do to take on a more important role. Feeling that he could have no impact, particularly on his mother, was a source of angry frustration. Yet George felt afraid to express those angry feelings. He felt insecure about his emotional connections. Anger put him at risk—he believed he might lose the little love and attention that came his way. Unable to take such a chance, George became the reverse—the quiet guy, the person nothing ever really bothered. But buried frustration doesn't simply disappear; often it surfaces indirectly. So, though confrontation and angry outbursts weren't his responses he would invariably and unconsciously do something "accidentally" that served to get back at his family. Without his realizing it, things such as forgetting and making mistakes became his passive way to express anger. The feeling that he can have no effect, particularly on women, and the buried frustration over his impotence play important roles in George's partnership with Helen.

IS THIS YOUR HUSBAND'S PAST?

Though your husband's personal history may vary somewhat from George's, his past may reflect a similar need. To help you clarify these connections, see if these descriptions apply to your husband's upbringing.

He sensed his parents were disappointed with him. He was the wrong sex, looks, or brains, came too early or too late, was adopted or illegitimate.
A child who senses he started life on the wrong foot may feel powerless as an adult—as if nothing he can ever do or achieve will alter his first indelible impression.

He wasn't a real troublemaker, just klutzy, inept, forgetful, and sloppily careless.
Early in life, he learned that direct confrontation was dangerous, carrying the risk of rejection. Instead, he developed subtle and passive ways of demonstrating anger. This indirect assault on people—getting under their skin—is carried into adulthood.

He always had friends, but was never the leader of the pack. He preferred the backseat.
As a kid, he never saw himself as a prime mover. As

an adult, he still doesn't, choosing instead a position on the periphery of relationships.

George's parents wanted a girl when George was born. Perhaps your husband had siblings close in age. Perhaps he was not considered the outstanding child. One sibling often casts a shadow another sibling lives under. This may have left your husband feeling insignificant, as if nothing he could do could earn him his own place in the sun. Your husband's parents probably never applauded his achievements. And the feeling that nothing he accomplishes makes a difference still lingers in him today. Your spouse may have a sense that family and friends cast him in a certain image, which supports his unconscious view that no matter how hard he tries he can't make people think different about him.

Was your husband's mother the dominant force at home while his father generally withdrew? This imbalance of power may have served as a model for his own adult relationship with a woman. Like his father, your husband may assume he must cede power to you, his wife. Your husband's parents may have seemed to him self-involved—in their work, troubles, each other—which made him feel he couldn't reach them, so he gave up trying. As an adult, he still assumes he can have no effect. His parents may have been opinionated, stubborn, fanatic. A parent whose mind is closed locks out a child and never helps him develop a sense of his own effectiveness.

If your husband was the good boy, the easygoing child like George, his anger and frustration probably remain submerged. Your husband's past has taught him to express his frustration in passive, irritating ways that satisfy his need—but threaten your relationship.

HELEN'S PAST

Self-reliance is a trait Helen was forced to acquire quickly and prematurely. All of a sudden, her father, a vigorous, outgoing man in his late thirties, died of a massive heart attack. This unexpected shock overwhelmed Helen's family. She can still vividly recall her mother sobbing behind a locked bedroom door. When her mother finally emerged she had little energy for eight-year-old Helen and her little brother and sister. Absorbed in her own grief, Helen's mother was emotionally unavailable to her children; Helen felt also abandoned by her. It was as if both parents had died. As the eldest Helen tried her best to fill the gap for her siblings. She became, as her grandmother nicknamed her, Little Mother to Melissa and David. By junior high school she was spending afternoons helping out in the hardware store her father had left. Early on it became clear that Helen, not her mother, before long would be running the business.

Convincing herself that "I'll have time later," Helen never pursued her vague plans for college. Time for other things never materialized; even boys took a backseat to her "taking care of everybody." Taking care included seeing Melissa married and David off to college.

While Helen never asked for thanks, she realized her brother and sister took her for granted. Her giving was a one-way street—neither of them would have ever come through the way she did.

Having to take on an unusual share of responsibility early in life had a profound effect. The actual loss of her father and the emotional loss of her mother made Helen's survival dependent on one thing—Helen. Independence became a way of coping with loss and preventing life from erupting into chaos. For Helen, the world was not an orderly place; life could change dramatically and unexpectedly. It was through these experienced circumstances and the belief that life was not stable that Helen (like any child who might feel a lack of parental support) was driven to rely on herself alone. Mistrust was a lesson learned early. It is a feeling, as an adult, she cannot relinquish.

When she was twenty-two, Helen met George on a blind date. She was impressed with his gentleness. "Whatever I wanted, he wanted. We seemed so compatible. Even with sex, he knew if he pushed even a little I'd give in, but he never did. And there was never any question of my giving up the business." George, a man who let Helen take control, felt like the right man. Six months later they were married.

IS THIS YOUR PAST?

Could your past have created a need in you similar to Helen's, a need to rely on no one? Here are some of the elements that may have been part of your childhood, creating your need to be self-reliant.

You were the "little mother," serious and responsible. While still young, you worked, saved money, watched out for your siblings.

The position of authority you were forced to assume too early created the fear that your world would fall apart if you didn't take over. These fears follow you into adulthood, making it hard for you to ever let go of your independent position.

Without your father, your mother couldn't function (or vice versa).

Having a parent who is overwhelmed is a frightening experience for a child. It leaves you feeling that if something goes wrong with half the team, your whole world will go under.

None of your siblings took care of things. They always expected you to come through.

As a result, you feel that things work only when you're in charge—and that no one can be counted on to come through for you.

Helen's father died suddenly. Perhaps you had a parent who was caught in a crisis, became ill, left home, or died. The helplessness you felt upon losing a parent (whatever the circumstance) created in you the sense that nothing or no one is a sure thing. Or perhaps your parents had a troubled relationship, so that you lived with a sense that things could fall apart. Expecting disaster can be as threatening as living through one. One way to cope with expected catastrophe is by making sure you can go it alone.

If you had a childhood like Helen's, you too developed self-reliance early on. Being overwhelmed as a child, it was your way to survive. As an adult, you may find it hard to rely on others lest it make you vulnerable to the helplessness you once felt and still fear.

George and Helen both feel a sense of irritation and ongoing conflict in their marriage. But they also share mutual values and concerns, deep feelings—important things that give their relationship a foundation. The length of a marriage is no insurance against its dissolution. But if a marriage has a solid foundation, its strengths can be brought out through an understanding of the source of the conflict and each person's underlying needs.

DEBRA and SCOTT:
Beat the Clock

❧ ❦

Debra watched the elegant men in linen suits, the women in gossamer summer dresses and broad-brimmed hats mingling around her parents' swimming pool. The sun sparkled and danced on the water while waiters with white gloves served champagne. Debra, smiling wryly to herself, decided it was a perfect engagement party. She, as usual, had seen to every detail. Scott hadn't wanted a formal party. She still felt annoyed when she thought of Scott's response to the idea, "Deb, we've been living together. Why go to all the trouble to tell people what they already know? But if you want it, go ahead." Typical of Scott to take the party for granted and dump all the work in her lap, knowing she'd get it done.

Gazing about at this so-called perfect party, Debra felt the same old irritation with Scott creep up on her. She had been irritated even before the party began when Scott had thoughtlessly dropped wet towels on her party dress. Debra jumped as she felt someone kiss the back of her neck. Absorbed in thought, she hadn't noticed Scott approaching her. He spoke first, "I'm sorry about your dress, but really, Deb, don't you think you overreacted? Another time, you would have tossed the towel at me and laughed. Today you acted as if it was the worst thing I ever did to you. Some-

99

times I just don't know what to expect. You can explode over nothing. One minute I'm your best friend and the next you're barely speaking to me."

"It isn't the sin. It's the attitude," Debra shot back.

"I feel as if I spend all our time together apologizing, perpetually atoning," Scott went on, ignoring her jab. "Look, I'm even doing it now. I hate the sensation of falling in and out of your good graces."

Debra got furious. "You're all the same—just out for what you can get."

"Debra, I'm trying to smooth things over and you're jerking me around. I don't know how long I can take this."

"Break up with me then. It won't be the first engagement a man has broken. Now's the time to do it—before my father makes a toast."

"Debra, stop this; a fight today of all days. That's just what your parents would love. It's amazing: since their divorce they can't agree on anything except that I'm too young for you, that I'm not established enough, that I must be from the wrong side of the tracks since no one's laid eyes on my father in twenty years." Scott stroked her hair. "Come on, babe, I love you. You know how I feel about you. Why else would we be getting married? I know how important children and a family are to you."

Debra felt a lump form in her throat. She wanted Scott's children badly, but at thirty-eight, she wondered if she could still have them. And did Scott really want children? He was always commenting how cozy it was with just the two of them, how he wondered if things would be the same once children arrived. "I want to be a father—it's the kids I'm not sure about." Maybe it was his way of saying he didn't want to have children with her.

Scott kissed Debra. He could be so warm. He whispered, "I'll make it up to you in bed tonight." A warm, flushed feeling spread through her body; she felt color rise in her cheeks. Debra found her resolve to stay angry with Scott melting away. He pressed his body against her. "You do it to me, Deb—every time." Scott wasn't the least bit shy about telling Debra just how she made him feel; it made her tingle with embarrassment but it excited her as well. Her "perfect" party now seemed much less important than getting home and into bed with Scott.

A clinking of glasses interrupted Debra's thoughts. Across the pool her father and mother stood side by side, yet distant—each holding a glass of champagne in the air. The irony of the scene jolted Debra, "The phonies—they don't like each other and they don't wish Scott and me well either." Debra stiffened in Scott's embrace; bad thoughts, like unwelcome but persistent visitors, intruded on her good feelings. Despite his embrace, despite his words, she wondered again—was Scott's love the real thing?

DISCERNING THE PATTERN OF CONFLICT

Debra and Scott's conflict is powerful enough to mar the joy of their own engagement party—and to threaten their future plans. No matter how "perfect" the circumstances, Debra can feel taken advantage of by Scott and angry about it. Scott can feel trapped by Debra's moods and the volatility this creates in their relationship.

Debra and Scott are both clear about what they wish from this relationship: Debra to get on with marriage and family before it's "too late," and Scott to have a close and cozy relationship, with or without the benefit of a marriage ceremony. But because of the volatile nature of their relationship, both end up asking themselves, "Who needs this aggravation?" Their doubts mount: Debra wonders whether Scott wants her because it's comfortable for him, and Scott wonders whether Debra expects more than he can offer. And because of the age and social differences between them, their conflict is intensified by family disapproval.

But it's not social disapproval that keeps them frustrated; even Scott and Debra know that age difference can hardly be the real reason for a conflict. The true source of their discontent lies with their unconscious needs. Scott has a need to satisfy a craving to be loved. Without being aware of it, he wants a woman to take care of him, to be

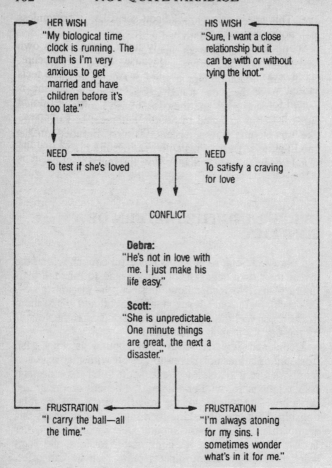

HER WISH
"My biological time clock is running. The truth is I'm very anxious to get married and have children before it's too late."

HIS WISH
"Sure, I want a close relationship but it can be with or without tying the knot."

NEED
To test if she's loved

NEED
To satisfy a craving for love

CONFLICT

Debra:
"He's not in love with me. I just make his life easy."

Scott:
"She is unpredictable. One minute things are great, the next a disaster."

FRUSTRATION
"I carry the ball—all the time."

FRUSTRATION
"I'm always atoning for my sins. I sometimes wonder what's in it for me."

attentive. This is why Debra, an accomplished, competent, somewhat older woman is his choice—each mothering gesture is proof that he is loved. Ironically, what looks like laziness to Debra is Scott's unconscious attempt to get more out of her, to secure another demonstration of her love. This craving can make Scott seem like a bottomless pit—nothing is ever enough.

Scott's craving for love neatly links with Debra's own need to test if she's loved. Because she feels insecure, Debra seeks a dependent man, like Scott. Though she feels wanted with such a man, she questions whether she is wanted for who she is or for what she does. This self-doubt drives her to test a man, to see if she is loved for herself. Debra is always on guard, acutely sensitive to the way a man treats her. Her insecurity easily makes her feel that her man fails the test. Her need appears as moodiness; it is expressed as the sudden and seemingly unprovoked withdrawal of affection. ("I've had it doing everything for you; it's time you pulled your own weight.") She is voicing the angry hurt she feels when she convinces herself she isn't loved unconditionally.

Debra's and Scott's needs create an emotional roller coaster: good moments pitch unpredictably into angry scenes; declarations of love quickly turn to threats of breaking up; calm and caring moments are overturned by doubts and accusations. Their needs, not their love, run them and their partnership. Their needs rob them of a carefree, joyful relationship.

IS YOUR HUSBAND LIKE SCOTT?

Could your partnership be like Scott and Debra's? Is one of you in search of mothering and the other willing to supply it but afraid of being used?

If your partner has a need to satisfy a craving for love, your complaints can illuminate his need.

Your complaint:
   "He always wants to stay home. He'd rather lie in front of the TV than go out. Getting him up and out to tackle chores is really impossible."
Your husband's need:
   Because he feels deprived of love, your man is in

quest of warmth and coziness. For him, there's no
place like home.

Your complaint:
"He's impossibly lazy."
Your husband's need:
Your lazy man is really a needy man. The less he
does, the more he gets you to do. He interprets your
efforts as a sign that you care.

Your complaint:
"He's sex starved."
Your husband's need:
With his need, the emphasis is on starvation rather
than sex. In every context, your partner hungers for
caring. It may make him seem sexually insatiable.

Your complaint:
"There's no reciprocity in our relationship; I do
everything." "He's always asking to use my car, bor-
row my records, and so on. We always spend my
money. He's a parasite."
Your husband's need:
Your man is not selfish—though he may appear to
be. His craving forces him to be a taker, leaving him
with few resources for giving. The intensity of his
need can leave you feeling exploited.

Your complaint:
"He's a bullshit artist. He knows how to get around
me."
Your husband's need:
Your spouse is desperate for you to respond to his
profuse expressions of affection. He tries so hard
that you are feeling that he is insincere.

Debra complains that no matter what she does for Scott,
it's never enough. You too may feel that your partner
always demands more and more. His need leaves him with
an intense longing that can never be filled. This can leave
you feeling as if he could suck you dry.
Perhaps you wonder why your man, who is such a success at work, is incapable of doing anything for himself

when you're around? This discrepancy is a clear sign of his need in operation. It takes a woman's presence to evoke his need to be nurtured.

If your man is anything like Scott, your vocabulary may be peppered with words like "lazy," "selfish," "irresponsible," "greedy," "user," and so forth. Try to understand the need his behavior reveals. This does not mean you must accept unacceptable behavior. It means you must try to uncover its source, which is the surest way to make things different and better!

ARE YOU LIKE DEBRA?

Are you unsure whether you are loved for yourself or for what you do for your partner? If you have a need to test if you are loved, your spouse will have expressed many of the complaints that follow.

Your husband's complaint:
"One minute she can be generous to a fault, and the next she'll suddenly insist that I pay—even if she's got more money than I do."
Your need:
Certain that you are being used, you need to see what reaction you evoke if you stop giving. But to your partner, your behavior seems arbitrary and evokes resentment from him. In this way, you end up fulfilling your own worst prophecy.

Your husband's complaint:
"Her usual ploy is to stalk off, drive away, or break up."
Your need:
For you, the best offense is a defense. Afraid of being abandoned, you do the leaving.

Your husband's complaint:
"She can make me feel as if I'm screwing a dead corpse. Even when *she* wants sex, she doesn't have an orgasm."

Your need:
Because you've convinced yourself that to him you're just "a receptacle," you act accordingly. Your mistrust of men destroys your ability to find men a source of pleasure and it acts as the obstacle to your own sexual fulfillment.

Your husband's complaint:
"She can get so angry that she'll look me in the eye and tell me she hates me."
Your need:
Your need is insidious—it can poison the feelings you have for your man.

Your husband's complaint:
"We can have great sex in the morning—and that night I'm not even allowed to touch her."
Your need:
With your need, sex is only a fragile alliance with a man. Great sex does not reassure you of his love. Instead, you feel that he loves you for the pleasure you can provide, not for yourself.

Scott complains that Debra is moody and quick-tempered. Does your husband complain about your short fuse, your volatility? You appear moody, but actually you are extraordinarily sensitive to feeling hurt. Your sensitivity can cause your partner to complain also that you get as cold as an iceberg. Whenever you feel hurt, you withdraw all your feelings, and to a man, this feels like the cold shoulder.

Does your husband say, "I'm accused of using her." You must understand that with your man's need, your feeling of being exploited is your own doing. You try so hard to please him and then convince yourself that that's the only reason he's interested in you.

Perhaps your husband complains that he feels as if you want him to jump through hoops. If he feels tested, it may be because you are constantly putting his love for you on trial. He may feel that you never really believe in his feelings for you and that you're always just waiting to find something wrong. For you, a man is guilty until proven innocent; your need makes you doubt his love. You are always on the lookout for signs that you aren't loved.

SCOTT'S PAST

Scott doesn't remember his father. "I was three months old the first time he left. He had a nine-month tour of duty on an oil rig—in Alaska or some place like that. He came back, but I guess a wife and baby weren't what he wanted. By my second birthday he had checked out permanently. I still have a few postcards he sent from time to time, but the last one arrived when I was five."

During Scott's first year, Scott's father supported his wife and child. "Even though my mother got his checks, she still had to work part-time. At first my grandmother took care of me. But I guess because my mother started to work full-time when my father's checks stopped coming, and I had begun to walk and was too much for Grandma, I was taken to a neighbor's every day. A Mrs. Bennett who was home with her own three kids. My mother told me there wasn't a day I didn't drag my tattered blanket over there. Anyway, I'm not sure, but I think that's the way it was until I started school."

What Scott remembers for sure are his mother's efforts to keep them going. "She was a legal secretary, and with all she knew and did she now would be called a paralegal. By the day's end she'd come home beat, especially if a case was coming to trial. She'd never tell me to leave her alone but I didn't bother her much. The only way I was a pain was about food. I ate too much—and I still do. I always needed another cookie or some more ice cream. I'm still not the sort of guy who can take one pretzel and put the bag away." Scott sums up his feelings by saying, "By this point I don't really give a damn about my father— frankly I'm probably better off without him. I'm not sure he'd have been the greatest influence on me. But I'm bitter about the kind of life he forced on my mother and me. She was so busy trying to survive that she couldn't even make the effort to find another man. Plenty of times she'd even apologize to me for not being able to be the kind of mother I deserved."

Scott's appreciation of his mother's plight and resignation over his father's absence obscure an important element of his childhood experience. Very early on his caretaking was interrupted. He was not neglected or not cared for but the intimate, nurturing bond was disrupted. His mother was there but she was busy, and sad (over her lost marriage), and regretful (about the limitations her life forced on her interactions as a mother). His father was not there at all. His grandmother was there but not young and vigorous enough to give fully to Scott what he needed. His neighbor was there but with three children of her own she was not as available to Scott as he may have needed her to be. Due to circumstances, Scott's caretaking was a case of unrealized potential. People were there for him but with their limitations. This childhood experience left him with an unconscious longing for more. A longing for the kind of total connection that seems to have always been just beyond his grasp. His longing brings him to a somewhat older, maternal woman like Debra—someone from whom he is unconsciously struggling to get more and more and more.

IS THIS YOUR HUSBAND'S PAST?

Is your man struggling with this longing for love, a longing that may have its roots in a past where love didn't realize its full potential? Is he trying to regain in his adult life what he may have lost as a child?

He was the child who worried about getting his fair share—the biggest piece of cake, the tallest glass of soda. He was always asking for things (toys, treats). He seemed greedy.
He wasn't greedy; he was anxious. A child who

doesn't get enough emotionally feels anxiety whenever he encounters an experience where "getting" is an issue. He may try to fill the emotional void materially. Since such substitutes don't satisfy the craving, the demand continues. It's this craving he may bring to your relationship.

He wasn't an excited, enthusiastic, curious youngster. He doesn't remember great moments in his childhood.
A child who isn't abundantly supplied with love and attention may lack the emotional energy to take life on. As an adult, he may look to you to take over.

Perhaps he was a thumb-sucker. Or he had an indispensable teddy bear or blanket. Or he was a fussy eater or overweight.
Children who miss nurturing often express their problems symbolically—perhaps through oral behaviors or by clinging to objects of comfort. As they grow into adults they may give up those behaviors or objects, but the neediness remains.

Scott doesn't remember his childhood very well. Though he can't put his finger on it, he feels his childhood wasn't a bad one, it just wasn't a content one. If your husband can't find the words to describe his childhood, the problems may have started early in his life, when feelings, not words, were the form of communication between child and caretaker.

When your husband was a small child, perhaps his family experienced separation, divorce, infidelity, illness, financial turmoil, or death. A family under stress may leave its caretakers with limited time, energy, or love. Unavailability is the root of longing.

Your spouse senses that his problems lie in relation to his mother (or caretaker), but he doesn't feel angry toward her. She wasn't bad or mean or neglectful. She was simply a figure of unrealized potential. A child's connection with his mother is his paradise. If something disrupts this, as it may have in the case of your man, he may increasingly try to restore it. Now, with you, he tries to plumb the depths of your giving. The problem is that no other woman can be someone else's lost mother or the mother who never was. If you feel he never has enough from you it may be because it's beyond your (or anyone else's) capacity to fill this role.

DEBRA'S PAST

Debra was nine when her parents divorced. As she recalls, "My parents' divorce overshadowed everything. Our home was never free from friction, tension, or arguments. Before they separated I can remember trying to be good, to be helpful, to make things better between them. After they split, I took on the job of peacemaker. As strange as this may sound I think I felt responsible for their failed marriage—as if I didn't do enough."

Debra's father compounded this feeling. Wanting to reconcile with his wife, he often used Debra as a messenger. "'Tell Mommy that Daddy wants to come home,' he'd say. I'd tell her, plus I'd tell her how different, how much nicer Daddy would be. At night I can remember crying desperately because nothing I did seemed to work."

Debra's efforts extended beyond her parents. Throughout her school years she was a doer, the teacher's pet, the friend to be relied upon for favors. Though she was well liked, Debra never believed her popularity. "In high school I'd chauffeur kids around from time to time. I would wonder if my friends liked me because I was one of the few girls with a car."

Boyfriends were another area of self-doubt. "What I liked was having a boyfriend—but not sex particularly. However, I would always go along with what a guy wanted. The first time I gave a boy a blowjob I was fourteen. I felt like dirt. Every time Ron called me I was sure sex was the only reason. I was scared he'd tell other boys. For the next year I couldn't help but be suspicious of anyone who'd ask me out."

Despite graduating at the top of her class, Debra didn't feel like college material. "I went to work as a secretary in a real estate firm where I met Jack, one of the agents. We lived together two years and were married for six more. Everything seemed so right until he walked in one day and announced he was in love with someone else, that I hadn't grown with him. It boiled down to the fact that he was bored with me."

In the painful aftermath of her divorce Debra swore no man would ever catch her off guard again. And this proved true. The next man in her life didn't walk out on her—he just used her. "The minute Enrique passed his medical boards I became unimportant. He blamed his residency training for taking up all his time but I knew it was just an excuse. The moment he got his license he became a big shot."

The turmoil in Debra's family life left its mark. The raging battle between her mother and father made Debra feel insignificant—neither seemed to have time or concern for her. In their anger and desperation they ended up using her as a go-between rather than paying attention to the pain she was feeling. The divorce itself underscored her feeling that she was not valued for herself: Debra felt not only abandoned but disposable, for if she had really mattered they would have stayed together. She had tried so hard to be a good girl, to mediate between them, to help save the marriage—yet she had been defeated. No matter how hard she tried, she was unable to control her life.

Her need to test whether she is loved for herself is rooted in this childhood riddled with doubt and insecurity. She needs the reassurance of a dependent man, like Scott. Yet each relationship becomes an attempt to try and prove she is loved for herself, not for what she does. Ironically, she works so hard at being in charge (as she did with her parents) that she ends up feeling as if Scott cares for her only because of what she provides. Regretfully, unless she begins to understand her need, their relationship may become a confirmation of all the unhappy emotions of her childhood.

IS THIS YOUR PAST?

Are you a woman like Debra whose childhood up-heavals created an adult who needs to test if she is loved? Here then are some of the characteristics of your past.

You remember crying, shutting yourself in your room, avoiding your house, wanting to be someone else's child.

These may be the reactions of a child trapped by family problems and feeling powerless. These diffi-culties may have left you with a fear of being vulner-able and helpless, which keeps you on your guard in adult relationships. Once hurt, you unconsciously swear, "Never again."

Your parents depended on you, confided in you, leaned on you—especially during a crisis.

Distraught parents may thoughtlessly burden a child, leaving the child feeling more useful than loved. This feeling may lie at the heart of the self-doubt you have with men.

You didn't say no to friends and boyfriends.

A desperate or insecure child is unwilling to hazard further rejection and may feel it is too risky to say no.

Debra's life was overshadowed by divorce. Perhaps yours was too. Perhaps you lost or were threatened with the loss of someone close to you. Perhaps you were an adopted, or foster, or illegitimate child. Perhaps your childhood was chaotic, disorganized, disrupted, volatile. Any of these different situations can be experienced by a child as rejection. A child who feels she is of little value carries that damaging self-image into adulthood. In addi-tion, it is in a stable, predictable environment that a child's trust grows. Your early uncertainties may have led you to be unsure of people. Your childhood loss may have sown the seeds of adult insecurity.

As a child, you may have felt that the truth was kept

from you or that your were lied to or misled. Perhaps your parents "protected" you from the truth—"Daddy's just going for a few days." "The doctor won't hurt you." Even when motivated by the best of intentions, adult dishonesty creates mistrust in a child. This is a mistrust that you may carry into your adult relationships, making it difficult for you to believe in your man's sincerity and love.

BARBARA and STEVE:
Great Expectations

❮ ❯

"Three thousand dollars? You've obviously made some mistake. My husband discontinued his VISA card at least two months ago. Just go back to your records and call us when you've straightened this mess out! Goodbye."

Barbara slammed the receiver down. If only she could believe what she had said. It was true that Steve had torn up his credit card in front of her—he had promised to control his spending—but it would hardly be the first time he'd broken a promise about changing. Why did she get taken in all the time? Didn't she know better? Wasn't it predictable? How many times had she told her therapist about Steve's disappointments? Why didn't it register? Promises. Promises. He could talk a good line but he never produced. Barbara thought of Steve's job—his entire career had been one false start followed by another. After fifteen years of marriage (and half a dozen jobs), his usual claim, "This time I know I'll make good, honey," had a hollow ring.

It hadn't always been that way. Steve may not have been high-powered, even when they first met, but he was so willing to try. He had jumped at Barbara's suggestion that he take night courses after work. When he dropped out in the second semester Barbara felt disappointed, but she couldn't protest—Steve had wanted them to have more time together. And so what, she had thought, a degree doesn't buy success. A man with Steve's looks and brains could become a winner any way he tried. And Steve always seemed a potential winner. Barbara remembered how receptive Steve had been to the plans they'd dreamed up together. He could be so romantic. Recalling her naïveté, Barbara laughed ruefully. She had believed in him then. Over the years she had gone from wholehearted faith to gnawing doubts and finally to bitter disgust. The things she had once been fondest of were now the greatest source of irritation. Take something as simple as shopping. Barbara had once been the envy of her newlywed girlfriends. Steve had been the only husband who'd set foot in a supermarket to do the weekly shopping. It was fun—at first— their togetherness. Now seeing Steve walking down a grocery store aisle enraged Barbara. "It's the only thing he's good for," she thought. "If he were a vice president of his electronics company instead of a salesman, he wouldn't have time to spend in a supermarket and he'd have money to pay for his damn charges."

If she let herself, Barbara's mind could race on. Life with Steve was an emotional roller coaster. It made her head throb to think of it—hope and disappointment, hope and disappointment, up and down, up and down. The pounding in her head grew worse.

The phone rang again. Barbara clenched her teeth and grabbed the receiver. What mess was it this time? she wondered. As if he hadn't a care in the world, Steve's voice piped up on the other end, "Hi, hon. Tried you earlier but the line was busy. What's doing?" Barbara exploded. "What's doing? You fuck off. Don't hon me as if everything is hunky-dory. I'll tell you 'what's doing.' I was on the phone hearing about your damn charges. You trot off to your so-called job and leave me to be humiliated by a collection agency because you spent three thousand we don't have and you don't earn. Throwing out the VISA card in front of me—what a laugh. You and your goddamn promises. You phony lying shit."

Steve's voice lost any trace of its sunny calm. He slammed back, "You bitch. You must have welcomed the call. What great ammunition. It's been at least a week since you could remind me that I'm a loser. Too bad the kids are in school, so they have to miss out hearing what a 'swell' guy their dad is." Barbara shot back, "It is too damn bad. I want them to know every single detail, so they don't end up washouts like you."

"Barbara, you're a steamroller. Nothing stands in your way. The kids' feelings—Ha! They don't matter. They don't even exist as long as you can vent your spleen. You're going to pay for it. Roger's only eight and he's scared of you already. Do you think he stammers because he's a happy kid?"

Barbara started to shake. Steve knew it killed her to think that the kids didn't love her, that they wouldn't turn out all right. He was being vicious. She couldn't let him know he had brought her to tears. She kept quiet. "No response, sweetheart? We know with you, no cat's got your tongue. Well, let me take advantage of this uncustomary silence of yours. I was calling to tell you that I'd gone over the sales quota this month. Don't ask me why I even thought of sharing the good news with you. I don't know why I still bother trying. Did you ever see your face when I'm telling you something? You look like you just got a whiff of rancid milk. They probably invented the word 'disdain' to describe your expression. Do you know what it means to live with a woman who's impossible to please? No matter how hard I've tried, it's never been enough. I don't know why I waste my breath. If you think I'm coming home tonight so you can unload more of this crap on me, you're crazy. You don't know how to be happy."

"Happy? What about your family's happiness? Did you think about that when you got that secretary pregnant? I don't know what's more revolting—knowing you screwed around or knowing you're stupid enough to bounce a check to her abortion clinic so every bank teller in town knows you're a shit. Don't come home. Who gives a damn."

"There are plenty of other women in this world— plenty." Steve slammed down the receiver. Barbara stood holding the phone. It was typical: confront Steve with his failings and he'd cut out, drink, play cards, not come

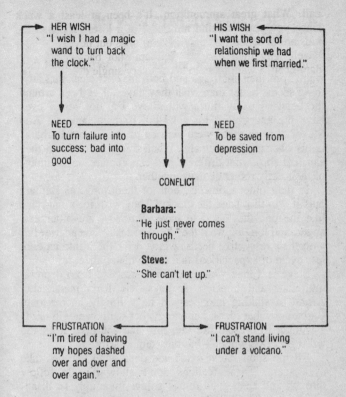

HER WISH
"I wish I had a magic wand to turn back the clock."

HIS WISH
"I want the sort of relationship we had when we first married."

NEED
To turn failure into success; bad into good

NEED
To be saved from depression

CONFLICT

Barbara:
"He just never comes through."

Steve:
"She can't let up."

FRUSTRATION
"I'm tired of having my hopes dashed over and over and over again."

FRUSTRATION
"I can't stand living under a volcano."

home. Barbara could only imagine what Steve was muttering to himself. "I'll find a woman tonight, a woman who won't be on my back." She'd heard it before. If she had the energy or the desire, Barbara could hate Steve. But she felt so ugly after one of their battles. It was ugly and exhausting. Her marriage was wearing her out. This last roller coaster ride felt like one too many. It was time to really think about getting off.

DISCERNING THE PATTERN OF CONFLICT

In the wake of a fight, ask Steve and Barbara what they want from their marriage and both make it clear that anything seems better than what they have. "I've been around the bend so many times with Steve I'm not sure I even have the energy left for a wish," Barbara laments. And Steve? "I wish that I were married to anyone but Barbara" is his overriding sentiment. When things calm down they can feel somewhat different and can conjure up an image of their early romantic days together.

In their quiet moments, both of them long, as Barbara puts it, "to turn back the clock." They wish for a marriage like the one they used to have. But why are bitterness, anger, and longing what they have instead? The answer lies with their respective needs, which drive them into an endless cycle of expectations that fail to materialize.

Steve is a man who needs to be rescued from depressing, sad, and hopeless feelings. He feels inadequate. Afraid of sinking into despair, he willingly latches onto Barbara and her ideas, her energy, her willpower. He needs a woman to breathe life into him and she does it all too willingly. This works—but only temporarily.

All too soon, Steve's sad and depressing feelings take over again. These feelings don't allow him to follow through and keep good things going. Invariably he disappoints himself and Barbara, sinking back into a sense of his own inadequacy. And the woman who was his source of hope becomes the intolerable reminder of his misery.

And Barbara? She is a woman who has an extraordinarily powerful need to transform bad into good, failure into success. She is attracted to Steve because unconsciously she sees his shortcomings and limitations as things she can turn around and undo. Barbara prods and pushes because she needs to remake her man and, through him, her life. Unconsciously she believes that Steve, a man, is her key to happiness, her potential redeemer. He is the raw material she will fashion into her Prince Charming. Every time

Steve takes up one of her suggestions, Barbara expects him to fulfill the unspoken promise that things will be different, that things will be better. When Steve doesn't change, Barbara's hopes are dashed; her secret prayer for happiness has gone unanswered—once more. In the wake of this pain she turns her angry disappointment on Steve.

Steve and Barbara are a man and woman who have enormous and excessive expectations of each other, expectations that cannot be met and that leave them in a bitter cycle of disappointment.

Uncovering these powerful needs can turn even these terrible feelings around. The pain of bitterness can be softened by the glow of insight.

IS YOUR HUSBAND LIKE STEVE?

Could yours be a relationship burdened by great expectations? Unconsciously your husband may have assigned you the task of rescuing him from despair while you cast him as the vehicle for your happiness and success.

Consider how he irritates and aggravates you. Behind each complaint you can see his need at work.

Your complaint:
  "He starts off gung ho but never comes through."
Your husband's need:
  Your enthusiasm lifts him up and gets him going. But his own sense of sadness and inadequacy eventually catches up and gets him down. Good feelings that last must come from inside, and he just doesn't have it in him.

Your complaint:
  "He gambles . . . drinks . . . does dope . . . runs around . . . overeats . . . smokes."
Your husband's need:
  A man struggling with bad feelings may try just about anything to drive them away. He depends on a "rush" of good feelings to erase inadequate feelings —for the moment.

Your complaint:

"As soon as I point out his problems he gets furious; I'm a bitch, a shrew."

Your husband's need:

For him a problem isn't just a problem, it's a sign that he's miserably inadequate. Unable to tolerate the feeling of self-hate, he gets furious with you.

Your complaint:

"He stalks out . . . doesn't come home . . . locks himself away . . . goes off with the guys . . . finds a hooker . . . has a one-night stand."

Your husband's need:

He sees in your face a mirror image of the disappointment and disgust he feels with himself. He can't tolerate this reminder so he runs from it.

Your complaint:

"Promises! Promises!"

Your husband's need:

He's not just lying to you; he's lying to himself. He's a man who wants to be different but feels he can't be different, and he's unwilling to admit that to you or to himself.

Barbara has often felt that Steve doesn't tell the truth, that he exaggerates or omits telling her things. "I don't trust what he says" is her refrain. Steve is simply coloring reality as he'd like it to be rather than as it is. Perhaps your man also gets caught up in his wishful fantasies as a way of denying the true state of affairs.

Money may also be used in the service of this denial. Does your husband overspend as Steve does? Does he tip too much; does he drive an expensive car? When a person feels woefully inadequate, he may act "the big spender." He needs to make others believe he's on top of the world; he needs to look big because he feels small.

Money may cause you frustration in other ways. Your husband may be financially disorganized: he owes money, lets bills slide, lends money and doesn't collect, has a poor credit rating, misses tax deadlines. As Barbara complains, "Steve's most overused line is 'It's in the mail.'" A man who believes he's inadequate may not take hold of his life —he's waiting for someone to take over and rescue him.

At times a man like Steve may seem manipulative. Barbara hates the sense that "he's out for what he can get." Do you, too, feel exploited? When you're really enraged, do words like "parasite," "leech," "selfish bastard," run through your mind? If your husband is like Steve, he is desperate; he'll pursue anyone or anything that promises to make him feel better—quickly. It may make him act the opportunist. He latches on to any opportunity for an "emotional fix." Obliterating his sense of inadequacy is his first priority. It can leave a woman feeling used.

If your husband and Steve seem to share a common style, you're probably accustomed to calling him a "bum," "wimp," "loser," "liar," "good-for-nothing." But take a chance—look beyond the labels and see his need at work. See the sadness, the despair that lies beneath the surface. Your understanding can make the difference.

ARE YOU LIKE BARBARA?

Do you, like Barbara, need to remake your husband? Perhaps the hidden agenda in your marriage is your turning things around. Living "happily ever after" may seem guaranteed only if you can turn a frog into a prince. Analyzing your spouse's frustrations and his grievances may clue you in on this need.

His complaint:
   "She never lets up. She wants me to be someone or something I'm not."
Your need:
   You can't stop the pressure because you need him to be different, to be better. You need him to make everything come out alright.

His complaint:
   "Why is she furious when I fail? My mistakes are considered federal offenses."

Your need:
Your man's failure is your defeat. It's a painful reminder that your dreams are shattered.

His complaint:
"She's a bitch."
Your need:
Your need makes you relentless. It may make you
seem hard and angry when you are trying desperately
to grasp happiness.

His complaint:
"I get a raise; she says ask for more. I get a job; she
wants me to get a promotion. I get a high school
diploma; she pushes for college."
Your need:
Your expectations of a man are extreme. It may
make a man feel as if nothing he does is enough, and
with your need—he's right.

His complaint:
"According to her I'm a lousy provider, a lousy busi-
nessman, and a rotten example for the kids."
Your need:
Extreme reactions demonstrate your need. It is so
critical for your man to make it that if he falters all
seems lost. Emotionally all your eggs are in one bas-
ket—his.

Steve's complaints extend to the bedroom. "It's 'Don't
touch me there,' 'Do this,' 'Don't do that,' or 'You come
too fast.' Who wants to fuck a traffic cop?" Barbara is
unwittingly trying to create the consummate lover who'll
give her the ultimate orgasm. That's her unconscious view
of a woman's happiness: a woman's bliss arrives in the
form of a man made perfect. Could this be what you strive
for when you make love?

Think of the number of times you correct your husband;
give him advice, suggestions, criticism, pep talks, second
chances; and push opportunities, promotions, job changes,
educational advancement. Steve accuses Barbara of acting
like his coach instead of his wife. If your husband also

feels that you are always pushing him, he may be resenting your need to renovate your man. He may feel angry at what he must sense is your lack of acceptance. And in fact, you are unable to accept him, for this would leave you feeling that you had given up your chance for real happiness.

Barbara is very sensitive to anything Steve says about their children. "She gets apologetic if I tell her that one of the kids is having problems—like trouble in school or not getting along with friends." Perhaps you, too, have a low tolerance for thoughts that your children may be unhappy. Without being aware of it, you want their lives to come with guarantees. You unconsciously desire perfect happiness for your children as well as yourself. The ordinary trials and tribulations of a child's life may feel unbearably unsettling. You may unconsciously see them as disasters, instead of as the bumps and bruises that are part of growing up. But life doesn't have to be so tense or disappointing. You can take steps toward this freedom by discovering your hidden needs.

A Note:

A relationship burdened by excessive expectations may be volatile. Cursing, yelling, threats, or even physical abuse may be regular and recurring features. The pain of disappointment is so devastating that we respond by lashing out. We can become enraged by a world that seems to frustrate our deepest hidden desires. Our pain causes our anger.

STEVE'S PAST

"My mother had me late in life, seven years after my sister. But I was no love child—I was an accident. My parents were separated when my mother got pregnant; it forced my father back home. Because of me they stayed together, on and off, for five more miserable years. Finally, when I was just starting kindergarten they split—permanently."

Though he was only five at that time, Steve has vivid memories. "There were custody battles, fights over who should get us kids when, arguments over money for support. It just never let up. And all the time my mother talking about my father, how lousy he was, how miserable he made her. She'd get on these crying jags. I hated it but I listened; I felt sorry for her too.

"Sure it all bothered me, but I handled it. You know how kids are with divorced parents. I knew how to get what I wanted from them."

Steve is bitter.

"With the help my parents gave us, we might as well have been living in an orphanage. I know my sisters felt that way; as soon as they could, both moved out and got married. I was stuck alone with my mother for years. At least then things got better. My mother gave me anything I wanted. It still drives my sisters crazy the way she spoiled me. You should have seen them after she bought me my motorcycle."

For Steve, school was somewhat better than home. "I loved Mrs. Lesser, my sixth grade teacher. She took a special interest in me. I think if she had told me to fly off the roof, I would have. Around Christmas I got in trouble for taking things that belonged to other kids, but Mrs. Lesser got me off the hook. She was a pushover for me.

"By high school, girls were more important to me than school itself. I can remember Judy Anderson, my first really serious relationship. She wanted an I.D. of mine to wear. I borrowed from everyone just to be able to buy it. I even hocked my bike so I could get a real silver and gold one. When I saw her wearing it, I felt like a million dollars.

"When Judy broke up with me, I went off the deep end. I smoked a lot of dope and drank a hell of a lot of beer. It really fucked me up. I never did well in school after that. I just got high and got by. That's why meeting Barbara was so good. After bouncing around for so long, I really felt as if with her I could make a new start. I really cleaned up my act with her."

Steve is an emotional orphan. From the day he was conceived, he was a burden, an intrusion in his parents' lives.

Though he was fed, clothed, and taken care of, he was, in some fundamental way, abandoned. This sort of early abandonment creates an indelible mark—it left Steve feeling inadequate, insignificant, sad.

It also created a *survivor*. With so little given to him, Steve learned early on how to endear himself, how to get the most out of anyone or any situation. It was the only way to escape his sad feelings.

This need to get an infusion of good feelings from outside himself is the driving force in his adult relationship. Unconsciously he turns to Barbara to save him from sinking into his dreaded feelings.

IS THIS YOUR HUSBAND'S PAST?

Could your partner be struggling with depressed and inadequate feelings? Perhaps as a child he got so little attention or support that as an adult he's always striving to fill the void and feel better.

As a teenager he tried drugs. He drank. He gambled. He tried to "lay every girl in sight."
During the turmoil of adolescence a child may seek the "quick fix" to obliterate sad and inadequate feelings. He desperately turns to activity that provides an escape, that creates the momentary illusion that there is no inner pain.

He liked to show off, impress people. He spent money on girlfriends, on a flashy car; he took chances; he bought favors.
A child who feels inadequate may try to look big in the eyes of his peers—as if to deny feeling small inside.

He was a "spoiled" child. His parents never said no. He managed to get what he wanted from them.

A spoiled child is a child who asks for more and more and is never satisfied. It may look as if he is trying to get material possessions, but what he is actually trying to get more of is love.

Steve readily acknowledges that he was "messed up," that his family life was troubled from early on. Looking back, your man may feel bitter about his childhood ("They fucked me up," or "I got a raw deal"). Or he may dismiss early pain as unimportant ("It's in the past," "What's done is done," or "Chalk it up to fate"). Those conclusions may prevent him, and you, from acknowledging the impact of that past. Family chaos, unhappiness, or trauma, particularly early in a child's life, can leave a child feeling unnurtured, unwanted, and unloved. Your man may be carrying around inside of himself that sad legacy of emotional abandonment.

BARBARA'S PAST

"I never saw my father play football, but I often imagined him in his uniform, holding his helmet under his arm —the way he looked in his college yearbook picture. However, a torn ligament prevented him from becoming a pro. It happened at the end of his senior year at college. If he hadn't been offered a coaching job at Wingate Prep School by his friend Ted Dimond, he would have really been stuck.

"When I was a kid, Mother's most overtold dinnertime story was about being wined and dined by big league scouts. She was engaged to Dad then and the scouts were really courting him. Mother always told the story the same way, verbatim. Mother got very excited—she had practically memorized the menus. Of course, she never omitted mentioning my father's injury. Dad would sit like a stone. I always wondered about that.

"In those days, my mother didn't seem angry that things

didn't pan out—it was as if she felt sorry for my father, and maybe herself too."

But Barbara has other memories.

"Later on it was different. My mother didn't have many interests or many friends. She devoted a lot of time to me. Ballet, piano, trips. You name it, I had it. My brothers resent it till this day. My mother had lines like 'A girl has to have what it takes,' 'It takes work to get the right sort of fellow,' or her all-time favorite, 'You're going to learn from my mistakes.'"

Over the years Barbara's mother became angrier and her father became more withdrawn. "Dad always drank, but by the time I was fourteen, it wasn't just social drinking." Barbara learned how serious the problem was in a painful way.

"I came into the house and my mother was shouting. 'Do you think any school but Wingate would keep you in this condition? Ted Dimond hangs on to you because he still has visions of you as the college star. He and you are the only ones who don't know you're a has-been—and a drunk to boot.'

"I don't think I ever forgave my mother for that. In fact, it was after that fight that Dad's drinking got worse. I swear my mother drove him to it.

"My father is a really decent guy. If only my mother could have been more understanding. But to this day my father takes her insults and swallows them. It's disgusting. Actually, it was disgusting for me too. Kids are supposed to have a ball as teenagers—not me. My dad's drinking, my mother's complaints, my fights with her, and on top of that dating. I dated boys from Wingate. Half the time I think they just wanted to get in good with 'the coach.' The kids didn't know about his drinking; they just loved him. By my senior year I had stopped dating. I counted the days 'til I could get away from Wingate to some place where things would be different."

Barbara's family lives with a ghost, the ghost of an ide-alized magical and wonderful hero. Somewhere in the past lurks a vision that makes the real person—her father—

seem like a failure by comparison. In the wake of this
comparison, the family feels not merely regret, but painful
disappointment and defeat. It is as if the possibility of de-
livering happiness to his family was the ball her father carried, the ball he fumbled and dropped.

In particular, Barbara's mother conveyed a feeling that
happiness would have been within the family's grasp "if
only" the promise, the potential, of a man had come true.
Her mother's lack of drive and ambition underscored this.
Barbara never developed a sense that success could be a
woman's personal accomplishment—it could only be
achieved vicariously.

Her mother's message was that a woman's life is not in
her own hands, is not under her own control. Instead, she
must be lucky enough to find a man to ensure her success.
In order to get the odds in her favor, a woman must work
on her looks, talent, intelligence, wit. But these aren't
achievements, they're improvements—a means to an end.

Barbara learned another lesson from her parents. Barbara felt sorry for her father and angry with her mother,
believing that with another, more understanding woman he
would have, in fact, come through. All this unfolds in Barbara's own marriage. This is the hidden agenda of her relationship. Happiness will come through a man and, unlike
her mother, she *will* make the dream come true. She will
succeed where her mother couldn't.

This brings her to Steve, a man with potential; he is the
raw material for her unconscious dream. She needs him
because she needs to turn failure into success.

IS THIS YOUR PAST?

Did you grow up to feel as if you had to fashion your
happiness out of a man's life? Would your father have been
the key to happiness "if only" things had been different? Is
this past the one you are unconsciously burdened by in
your marriage?

Your father was a man with a "great" past or "great"
promise. He was once athletic, popular, creative,
famous, well-to-do, successful.

You may have lived with an ideal image of your father's past. His "real" self may have seemed pale by comparison, leaving you feeling that your father was a case of unrealized potential. Unconsciously, you may be striving to realize that potential with the adult man in your life, your husband. He may have to be the ideal your father never could be.

Your mother was critical of your father. He was "henpecked."

It hurts to see a father humiliated, cast as a failure. As a woman you may be trying to undo this pain by turning your man into a success story. You are unconsciously trying to rewrite history—this time with a happy ending.

Your mother always talked about the good old days.

A mother's nostalgia over missed opportunities and broken promises may leave a girl feeling as if she too runs the risk of passing up happiness. This may be why you're always pushing, driving, working. You may be frightened into feeling that to relax is to allow happiness to simply slip by you.

Barbara remembers the attention her mother paid to her upbringing. She was always being ferried to lessons, classes, trips, parties. Ironically, despite all the chauffeuring, her mother never discussed or expressed interest in Barbara's own ambitions, goals, or future plans—with the exception of the goal of "finding a good man." Perhaps you learned what Barbara did: self-development isn't for you yourself, it is only to make a woman a more attractive "package." The goal isn't personal achievement. It's the insurance policy a woman takes out on herself to guarantee future happiness.

In some way, Barbara's mother lived vicariously through Barbara. "Sometimes I didn't know who was more excited about my dates—me or my mother. She would insist on meeting my boyfriends, tell me how to dress, question me all about my dates." Barbara sensed from her mother's overinvolvement that her mother's life had been less than she expected. Barbara was her way out. She offered her mother a sort of second chance, a way to make up for her own frustrations. This conveyed an important message: unless a woman watched out for it, life would be a series of disappointments at the hands of a man. Perhaps you too carry the burden of your mother's dreams that didn't come true. Your past may have left you with an urgent driving force—to make your life "the once upon a time that finally lived happily ever after."

RUTH and DAN:
Married to Mr. Goodbar

❧ ❦

Aaron Farr, her husband's law partner, was on Ruth's left.
As usual he was talking a blue streak. Not that Ruth heard
a word. How could she when inside she was burning with
humiliation. Sitting across the table, Dan, her husband—
acting as if she didn't exist—whispered into another
woman's ear what had to be, "Let's have drinks later."

It was unbearable; he never let up—even at an American Bar Association convention, surrounded by people
they both knew well. And it was disgusting the way
women went for it—as they always did. Suddenly Ruth
had the urge to hurl her wineglass across the table and see
it smash into both of them. The violence of her own
thoughts frightened her. How could she get so worked up?
But when Dan did this to her she felt as if she became
someone else, someone she didn't recognize. The feelings
were unbearable. Shaking with anger, Ruth felt herself getting sick. She had to go up to their hotel suite and lie
down.

If only one night she could go to sleep and wake up to
find it was a bad dream. But it wasn't. Dan had always
been a womanizer. Ruth knew his reputation even before
they met. But she had believed him when he had promised
things would be different if she'd marry him and have his
children. It was a joke—a bad joke—to recall that Dan

131

had been the one to urge marriage and above all kids. Why, when he had this insatiable need to score?

Sometimes Ruth felt that the only woman he didn't need for sex was her. Two years earlier for several months he hadn't come near her. Despite Dan's protests that she was "looking for problems," Ruth knew there was another woman: one of his clients in a big divorce case had needed to meet with Dan a little too desperately, a little too often. She'd been proven right. When confronted, Dan had had an answer. "If you weren't such a cold fish, not to mention so damn depressed all the time, I wouldn't be looking for anyone else."

When he had responded to Ruth's accusation, Dan had seen only one thing in his mind—Ruth sitting in the living room, practically in the dark, clutching a drink, waiting for his arrival home from work, no dinner ready, nothing, just Ruth waiting. Sometimes, knowing what to expect, he just didn't want to open the door. He cared for Ruth, but it was other women not his wife who made him feel good, desirable. Ruth could be so obviously uninterested in him that he'd lose his erection when they were in the middle of having sex. The only good sex they had was after a fight. Dan often shouted at Ruth, "The only time you're alive is when you're furious with me."

As on other occasions, the argument over that affair had ended with sex and a relative truce. But not for long. Within a year Ruth again noticed Dan's lack of interest and confronted him. Like so many other confrontations, it erupted into a shouting match with Dan finally exploding, "I have herpes, so that's why we're not screwing. I don't want you to catch it." Ruth went after Dan screaming, "You sick miserable bastard, you're suddenly my protector after you've screwed every woman in sight. I hate you— go to your sluts—see if I care—maybe you can get it up with them." Dan smacked Ruth across the mouth and stormed out of the apartment, hardly feeling or looking like the cool, composed, and successful lawyer he was known to be. Probably no one who knew them could conceive of the fights that went on behind their closed bedroom doors.

The next morning Ruth had changed the locks. She

knew Dan's capacity for violence; it was the only way she could feel safe. She was through with him, she thought. Weeks dragged by. Most days Ruth found herself alone, consoling herself with a bottle of wine. One day drifted into another. As time dragged on, Ruth found it difficult to get up and dressed.

Pearl, her best friend (and about the only woman who had never responded to Dan's passes), had finally insisted she get out. "I'm not going to let you go down the tubes the way I did" was Pearl's refrain as she dragged Ruth out to an AA meeting. At Pearl's insistence, Ruth actually went to a few meetings, but then the phone calls came, day after day: Dan had to see her. Finally, when he arrived one midnight begging to be let in, swearing things would be different, Ruth opened the door. She'd been miserable without him. That night their lovemaking had been as wonderful as she could ever recall. And she remembered Dan's words, "Forgive me, Ruth. Nobody means anything to me but you. But the only time I seem to matter to you is when I'm not around." Ruth knew it was true. She'd try harder, too, to show Dan she really wanted him. They'd both try harder.

If only it had lasted. It seemed as if all it took was her week's vacation trip with Pearl to set Dan loose again. Coming back to find his passion for her cooled, Ruth knew she was back on the merry-go-round. Why did she let herself believe it would be different, that the abuse would stop?

And now, across the table was another humiliation to swallow. Ruth got up and excused herself to the others. Dan followed her. "Where are you going, Ruth? Aren't you going to stay for the dancing? It should be fun." Ruth didn't respond. "Ruth, don't do this to me. You know how important this dinner is to me." Important! She didn't give a damn for his big-deal legal career. For all she cared Dan could go off with this woman right now. Suddenly, with Dan at her heels, she bolted from the room. As she ran, Dan's voice followed, "Ruth, honey, are you all right?" No, she thought. She wasn't, he wasn't, nor was their marriage.

DISCERNING THE PATTERN OF CONFLICT

Ruth and Dan agree on one thing. "I'm a different person outside of my marriage. I hate the person I become in my own home. Things get ugly between us."

They both wish to remove this ugliness from their lives. Dan wants more than just peace and quiet. He'd like "a marriage with electricity. I want sparks to fly between us. I want a wife who knows I'm there, a woman who gets turned on."

Ruth above all wants peace and a marriage based on respect. "I don't want money, jewels, furs; none of those things matters. I just have to be married to a man who respects me and treats me as if he does."

Ruth feels a long way from this emotional goal. "Respect in my marriage? Are you kidding? As long as Dan's getting stroked, he doesn't care who's getting hurt—least of all me."

Similarly, Dan feels his wish eludes him. "I swear our marriage lost its sexual energy a week after our honeymoon. Ruth isn't really interested in me at all."

Ruth and Dan are aware of their wishes and all *too* aware of the frustrations that make those dreams seem so distant. But the sources of their conflict are anything but obvious. It may be the last thing you'd suspect, but despite Dan's style he is a man plagued by doubts about his own masculinity. Out of this insecurity emerges a need to establish his manliness, his virility. This puts him under a constant pressure to prove himself, hence his relentless pursuit of women. Each flirtation, seduction, or affair is an unconscious effort to confirm his potency, his power as a man. He is not trying to conquer women, but his own gnawing self-doubt.

And Ruth is a woman with deep inner pain—the burden of a brutally unhappy childhood—one of the walking wounded. It is a pain and sadness so grave that it threatens to engulf her.

Unconsciously she searches for a way to avert this threat

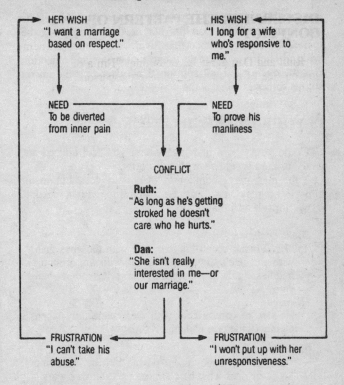

HER WISH
"I want a marriage based on respect."

HIS WISH
"I long for a wife who's responsive to me."

NEED
To be diverted from inner pain

NEED
To prove his manliness

CONFLICT

Ruth:
"As long as he's getting stroked he doesn't care who he hurts."

Dan:
"She isn't really interested in me—or our marriage."

FRUSTRATION
"I can't take his abuse."

FRUSTRATION
"I won't put up with her unresponsiveness."

of engulfment; she seeks to divert herself from her innermost feelings, to drown out the plaguing gnawing sadness within.

And together what cycle of conflict do these needs produce? Ruth's sadness leaves her without the energy to be excited about her life; in particular, it robs her of a capacity to be sexually alive and vital. Unaware of her sadness, Dan feels only her unresponsiveness; it threatens his already shaky sense of masculinity. Inevitably he seeks other "conquests" to prove himself. And Ruth is left enraged by his humiliation, his abuse, his abandonment. She experiences Dan as an inflicter of pain. In this lies a sad irony: infuriated with Dan, feeling victimized by him, Ruth forgets her own inner turmoil. Dan fits her need perfectly—he becomes the enemy outside that diverts her from the enemy within. Their needs create a cycle of anger and rejection. But the cycle need not spin on. Understanding the unconscious forces at work is the way out.

IS YOUR HUSBAND LIKE DAN?

Could yours be a marriage where you feel abused and your husband is riddled with self-doubt?

Your man may seem quite macho to you, but inside himself he may very well be struggling with a need to prove himself as a man.

Your complaint:
"He'd rather spend his free time with the guys than with me. He's always going out with his drinking buddies, golf partner, and the fellas to a ball game . . ."

His need:
He's more comfortable with men, especially when their activities are undeniably "manly."

Your complaint:
"The women's movement passed him by. At home he never does what he classifies as 'woman's work.' He's definitely got a double standard."

His need:
Rigidity about sex roles is a sign he may be threatened by any perception that he's anything less than 100 percent macho. Crossing sex-role stereotypes is a scary leap—one he can't make.

Your complaint:
"He doesn't want a wife. He wants a harem. He shouldn't be married."

His need:
His need pressures him into completing the milestones of manhood; he doesn't want to be married, he *has* to be. His public image must say, "Here's a regular guy."

Your complaint:

"He's so jealous. I can't look at another man without an outburst. I'm not allowed to wear a bikini or a low-cut dress. He'd like me to dress like a nun."

His need:

He may resent your sexuality, your potential for arousing men. It forces him to think about other men who he believes have what it takes when he fears he doesn't.

Your complaint:

"He wants children, but the last thing on earth he is is a family man. He pushed for kids but he isn't mature enough to be a real father."

His need:

He may have needed children as a confirmation of his potency; he needed to "father," rather than to be a father.

Ruth gets furious because Dan is relentless; he flirts with every woman he sees. If your husband seems to have a relentless, indiscriminate, constant, or compelling need to sexualize relationships with women, he is demonstrating a need to prove his masculinity. He may try to quell insecurity through sexual conquests, as if to say in the wake of each victory, "I'm irresistible, I must be *all* man!"

Ruth has often been embarrassed by Dan's remarks about "fairies," "faggots," "fruitcakes." You may be aware that your husband is very put off by homosexuality; perhaps his language is also peppered with derogatory remarks that embarrass you. He may hate "weak" men and idolize strong ones (football players, generals, and so forth). Perhaps you've even gotten annoyed when he teases your son about being a "sissy." A man struggling with his sexual identity may be intensely threatened by men who seem to reject their masculinity. One way to defend himself from people who threaten him is to turn them into reviled enemies, objects of ridicule—to call them names.

Regrettably, there's a dark side to Ruth's relationship: Ruth can even be frightened by Dan. "The way he can look at me, the things he can say. Sometimes I'm sure he despises me." Hate is an element of this need. It is as if the

presence of a woman he can't turn on, can't conquer, calls
his masculinity into question; a woman like this stirs his
self-doubt. You may wind up bearing the brunt of your
man's fury because you become the symbol, the reminder,
of his failings.

Perhaps it doesn't stop with words and looks. Does your
man have outbursts? Is he abusive? A man whose masculinity is always on trial feels there is something wrong with
him. Your partner may be a person who hates himself but
can't admit it; instead he turns on others—namely, you.

Remember something extremely important here. No
matter what roots it may have, abusive behavior is unacceptable behavior. There's a common misconception that
psychological understanding is a way to "get off the hook"
for our actions. On the contrary: *explaining behavior does
not mean excusing behavior.* No matter what psychological
factors are involved, violence is an unacceptable condition
for a relationship. Psychological understanding *is* the road
to making real changes in our lives. But along that road,
each of us—no matter the origin or nature of our conflicts
—is responsible for our actions.

ARE YOU LIKE RUTH?

Might you be engaged in a stormy, tumultuous, or even
terrifying relationship to save yourself from feeling your
deep inner pain? See if these complaints make sense to you
and explain your need.

His complaint:
    "Sometimes I think she *wants* to fight. She provokes
    the hell out of me. I'm the enemy."
Your need:
    You need to be fighting the outside enemy—your
    man—so as not to feel the inner one—your pain and
    sadness.

His complaint:
    "I can't win. She's got two moods—angry or de-
    pressed as hell."

Your need:
Calm, peaceful, quiet moments leave you vulnerable to hearing the voice of your inner pain. Kindness is a reminder of what you so sorely lacked growing up. What's more, in that silence, your sadness catches up with you.

His complaint:
"She has sex like it's her duty. Screwing her is like making it with a rag doll."
Your need:
A deep inner sadness robs you of the possibility for pleasure and sexual intimacy.

His complaint:
"She drinks." "She takes tranquilizers." "She takes sleeping pills." "She smokes dope."
Your need:
Obliterating the pain is the driving force in your life. These are some of the ways a person with your need anesthetizes her feelings. The misery is so powerful only a potent force can remove you from it.

His complaint:
"She won't give me a blowjob. Oral sex? Anal sex? According to her I'm supposed to go to a hooker for anything besides the missionary position."
Your need:
Through sexual rejection, you become a partner in your husband's infidelity. The eventual outcome? Antagonism, altercations, aggravation, and more. All of which leave you with little time or energy to focus on your inner feelings.

Dan feels undermined by Ruth, especially when it comes to his career. "She's blown plenty of important moments for me. I can never count on her." Are you frequently too tired, too sick, or too uninterested to be at important business functions with your partner? Or do you leave early with a headache? Or in a huff because he's not treating you properly? Several things may be at work. Perhaps depression saps your energy—it may paralyze your capacity to really care about anything he does. Or you may be trying to provoke your spouse. Getting him angry, and getting angry back, is your best defense against feeling sad.

You may be undermining your marriage in other ways. Do you exclude your spouse from important areas of your life? Is he shut out of your social life, hobbies, interests? Are you surrounded by friends he can't stand? Do you leave him out or behind, perhaps suggesting he doesn't have what it takes to keep up? Excising your spouse from major areas of your life may be your unconscious way of pushing him away, leaving him vulnerable to another woman's attention. Seeking an escape from your pain, you unwittingly play a part in the making of the conflicts that plague your relationship.

Unfortunately there can be even more extreme situations than this. Sometimes a woman may do more than just undermine her partner; she may humiliate her husband. Ruth, in a moment of pique, is not beyond this—she taunts Dan or puts him down. She mocks him about his career, dubbing him "the big-shot lawyer." Dan's sexual prowess is also her target. "I'm not proud of myself but I have told him I've had better lovers. I can't bear to admit it, but when I'm really feeling vicious I've even swiped at him for not being able to keep it up."

Why does Ruth lash out? In going for the emotional jugular, she is assured of a response—rage. And rage in a poorly controlled man may erupt into a violent, abusive act. An abusive relationship is a way—a terribly self-destructive way—of wiping out the memory of past misery. A woman engaged in a vitriolic, volatile, violent relationship is *always* a woman in deep emotional pain.

Perhaps your relationship has not reached this extreme; perhaps it has. Wherever you are on this continuum, you may have, regrettably, learned to dispel your pain in a self-destructive fashion. But this needn't be your or any woman's destiny. Absolutely not.

Every cycle, even the most self-defeating, can be broken.

This is a good moment to clear up what is a frequent misunderstanding about women trapped in abusive relationships.

No woman likes or wants to be abused. The problem is far more complicated. Hard as it may be to conceive, an abusive relationship is somehow a tactic for personal survival. The alternative of letting inner pain be felt is so threatening that it feels intolerable. Ironically, abuse is easier to tolerate. This is the big tradeoff: Abuse is tolerated so that overwhelming depression is warded off. If a woman tolerates such torment, it is a testament to how much bigger and more awful her burden of inner anguish must be. Abuse is the lesser of two evils.

Another point. No matter the nature or extent a woman may go to provoke a man, she is not to blame if abuse erupts. Never. The only person responsible for a violent act is the person who commits it.

DAN'S PAST

"Until ninth grade I was small and pretty shy. Kids used to tease the hell out of me. But my father helped me toughen up. If I came home crying he didn't cuddle me. Oh no! He'd get ticked off. 'What are you—a damn sissy? Knock some heads in and they'll shut up.' By the time I was twelve or thirteen nobody messed with me. I remember, in the seventh grade, in the locker room, a big guy, maybe a ninth grader, said something about 'little guys having little dicks.' He was a head taller than me but I decked him.

"My father was a card. All my friends liked him. He was a real regular guy, always ready for a good joke. He'd even sneak us into the garage and show us porno movies. He was no prude."

Dan's mother was very different. "My mother would get furious when we talked man talk. She'd just walk out of the room red in the face muttering, 'What kind of an example are you?'

"My mother's father was a preacher and Dad used to say, 'Your mother was sheltered; she didn't get to know all sides of life like I did. In her daddy's house anything but going to church and drinking tea was undignified.'

"My parents had very different backgrounds and very

different views on how to raise me. When it came to my sister, they were in perfect agreement—they didn't tolerate a foul word out of Karen's mouth, and if she wasn't in from a date by eleven, all hell would break loose. But over me they were always fighting. They really had it out over the Corvette Dad let me get in my senior year—he even kicked in half the money. To my mom it was a big waste of money and dangerous. My father got really mad at her. 'Do you want a pussy or a man,' he shouted. I got the car. I know my mother worried about me, but after that argument she didn't object in front of my father.

"My senior year was the best in my life. I loved that car. I fooled around with friends. We'd hang out in town or maybe drive to the shore. And girls just loved it. I can remember Margie Stonehall. We used to call her Coldstone because she was a real cockteaser and would never come across. Not with me. We'd park and she just loved to go down on me."

That relationship, like most of Dan's, didn't last long. "In all my dating I never liked getting tied up with a girl; I liked my freedom. It's just when all my friends started pairing off and there weren't so many guys to hang out with, it seemed time to settle down like all the rest. Ruth was someone I respected. She wasn't easy like so many women I'd met. She was fine. Actually I was the first and only man she ever slept with."

Dan's parents seem like a kind of "odd couple." His mother was prudish and repressed—trying to deny her own as well as her family's sexuality. By contrast, his father was full of macho talk, unable to forgo drawing continual attention to anything remotely sexual. Ironically, though they expressed themselves quite differently, both of Dan's parents were extremely uncomfortable with their own sexuality: his mother had to hide it, his father to flaunt it.

Dan has been affected by both, but particularly by his father. Sexual bravado was his father's way of masking doubts about his own manhood. His father's own self-doubt ultimately made him anxious about his son. Dan's father's insecurities prevented him from accepting Dan for what he was; the slightest suggestion that Dan wasn't "all man" (such as tears, nonaggressiveness, shyness, small stature) was intolerable.

Dan picked up the concerns, doubts, and worries; they became his own. He grew to reject as unacceptable and wrong any of his interests, traits, and characteristics that fell outside the macho stereotype. He grew into an adult preoccupied with his masculinity.

IS THIS YOUR HUSBAND'S PAST?

Is your partner trapped by self-rejection? Did he learn early on to actively deny a part of his own being, as if anything less that John Wayne was no man at all?

His father was "all man," pushing competitive sports, dating, toughness.

A father who is consumed with being a man and making his son into one is actually a father consumed by doubt and worry.

He spent his adolescence cruising, scoring, making it. He went through women. He was sexually active.

From early on intimacy may have been less important than scoring. He may have needed each sexual encounter—like a notch on a gun—to prove his prowess and potency.

He was competitive and a poor loser. As a teenager he had fights with other boys, especially if he was teased, slighted, or confronted.

From adolescence on, rage was his reaction to any challenge to his manliness, and insecurity made him perceive the slightest gesture as a challenge.

A double standard existed openly in Dan's family. Girls had to be "good" or risk punishment, and boys had to be "studs" or risk ridicule. Rigidity, especially about sexual mores, burdens children. Perhaps your husband, like Dan, felt he lacked permission to cross over the boundaries. He may not have wished to be sexually active but, fearing humiliation, may have been pressured into it. In his adult life, he may still act as if he's under such pressure.

Another childhood element may have contributed to a man's need to establish his masculine identity: early homosexual experiences. As a part of development, many boys engage in sexual play with other boys (for example, in mutual masturbation). For many men it becomes merely an accepted part of their growing up. Sometimes, however, it may become a terrible dark secret a boy carries into adulthood. If such a secret exists, disproving that he has anything but strong masculine urges may be its legacy.

RUTH'S PAST

Ruth can recall few pleasant memories about her childhood. "There were one or two nuns at school who were nice. And Judy Marchi, my best friend since fifth grade, was someone I had fun with—her father was a big drinker like mine—but that's about it."

The more powerful memory was of a home in constant turmoil. "Every single day of my life I'd come home from school, walk up to the front door, and listen for my parents' shouting. On a quiet day—if my father was out, at the local bar with his cronies or at the track—I could make it to my room. (Not that I had much peace there. Most of the time my sisters, Pearl and Bonnie, would invade—we all shared a room.) Occasionally, but I'm talking once in a blue moon, my mother might leave me alone upstairs. But she worked—at the school cafeteria—so she needed me to help with my sisters, or supper, or other things around the house.

"If my father was home, dinner was the worst. It sounds unbelievable but he once took a whole casserole my mother made, screamed at her for being a lousy cook, and hurled it across the kitchen. It smashed against the wall. My mother started to scream and cry. Pearl and Bonnie were frightened to death, so I took them out of the house to Judy's. (Thank God she knew my situation.) I didn't bring them home till really late—way past their bedtime. They were so scared they slept with me all night. I don't think I slept. I cried the whole time. We all got to school late the next day. We had to sneak out of the house—my father, as usual, was sleeping, or maybe passed out, on the living room couch."

Ruth was not always able to make such quiet getaways. "Look, my father hit me—plenty of times—and my mother too. Half the time he was so out of it I'm not even sure he knew what he was doing."

Her mother's tolerance of her father's behavior infuriated Ruth. "If my mother got me alone she'd spend hours talking about her rotten life. I begged my mother to do something—divorce him or just leave. Once or twice she packed us off in the car, but we never stayed away. Her excuse? 'You don't understand, Ruthy, it's not so simple. Where does a woman with three little girls go, Ruth?' Once I was old enough to realize she'd never do anything, I gave up asking.

"While all this was going on, my parents sent us to parochial school. It was a mixed blessing; it was a lot nicer than the local public school, but the nuns were impossible about anything that even remotely had to do with sex. That joke about not wearing patent leather shoes, so boys couldn't see your panties in the reflections, was no joke at St. Francis.

"And my father watched us girls like a hawk. We couldn't curse, we had to be very respectable. Some joke! And believe me, I took it all very seriously. I still am a believer. I don't think my teachers ever really realized the problems at home. My mother didn't let on about how bad things were—even our neighbor didn't catch on. I remember when Dad screamed, usually the first thing Mom did was run around the house closing the windows.

"You know, two of my uncles—my father's brothers—are alcoholics too, but for years everyone in the whole family tried to pass them off as having slight drinking problems. 'The Drew boys love their beer' was how my father put it. One of my aunts managed to leave her husband, my uncle Jack, but she didn't divorce him—they just lived apart.

"When I was eight, Jack moved in with us for a while. He was always bringing us treats. He'd make me sit on his lap before he gave me whatever he brought. This isn't easy to say—I've never told anyone—but he'd unzip his fly and make me touch his penis, and I did it and then he'd give me a gift. This went on for about a year. I never told my sisters about it, but I bet it went on with them too. My mother finally threw Jack out. She always maintained it was because he didn't contribute any money to the household. But I wonder—not that she ever said anything—if she got wind of what he was doing. I hate Jack. I haven't spoken to him in years."

Ruth's childhood was brutal. She was physically, emotionally, and sexually abused. She faced the constant humiliation of her father's drinking and the family's unhappy and disrupted life. And then there was her shame over her aquiescence to her uncle. The need to hide all this left her guarded and isolated—especially from her peers. (Only Judy with her similar suffering could be admitted into Ruth's life.)

Ruth was deprived of her childhood by the family problems that forced her to take on adult responsibilities. She was parent to her sisters and even confidante and adviser to her mother.

And her childhood innocence was lost in other ways. Her father's physically abusive behavior and her uncle's sexually abusive behavior conveyed an angry disrespect and disregard for women. Her mother's tolerance of abuse reinforced this notion—that a woman is worthless. As a result, Ruth grew up carrying within her a sense of degradation and self-hatred, which is a source of great pain.

Tragically, Ruth was forced to face her difficulties alone. Because of their problems, Ruth's parents were consumed with each other—so much so that they were oblivious to the sexual abuse of their own child. All their efforts, energy, and attention centered on the problems between them because of her father's drinking. They were two self-absorbed and self-involved people who had little if any emotional energy left over to nurture and protect their children.

The wound of Ruth's childhood is deep and raw. Inside her is a searing sadness and pain that threaten to overwhelm her. Like her mother, she becomes a man's victim in order to stem the emotional tide she fears may engulf her. She battles the "enemy" without to forget, for the moment, the pain within.

IS THIS YOUR PAST?

Might you be one of the walking wounded? Your past is the best clue to your present.

Your father or mother drank, took drugs, gambled, or ran around. They were physically or emotionally abusive.
Growing up in a home beset by these problems always leaves its mark on a child. No child walks into adulthood unscathed.

You were wild as a teenager. You had boyfriends who treated you rottenly. You screwed up in school. You were involved in drugs, drinking.
A child full of misery is likely to create for herself a miserable adolescence. The troubles outside mirror the troubles inside.

Your mother tolerated an abusive marriage.
Regrettably, this may have been a powerful model— one you carry on in your own marriage.

Not all girls with Ruth's need act out as teenagers. Ruth didn't. She cried alone. Perhaps that isolation describes your growing up years. Did you become depressed and withdrawn—even thinking about or attempt suicide? Were you anorexic? Sometimes a terribly wounded child turns against herself with this process of self-starvation or destruction.

Sexual abuse is an assault on a child that chases her into adulthood. It leaves the child feeling ugly, shameful, even "sick." If abuse is left a dark and "dirty" secret, the victim of it may feel as if the only way to cope with it is to drown out the bitter memory.

Thinking back—could Ruth's history in some way or other be yours?

Is this confrontation with such a difficult, even sordid, past disquieting? Depressing? Is the answer an inescapable *Yes?* Why say it? Because it is the first step toward escape —the first step to saying *no* to this painful cycle. And you're worth it!

JEAN and BRAD:
Wistful While You Work

ﻬ ﻬ

It was a game for Jean. She closed her eyes and ran her hands over Jeremy's body. First through his hair, then slowly over his eyes and his absolutely perfect nose. Then his shoulders. She loved the roundness—so smooth and hard. Down his chest toward his waist, so small compared to the bulk above, and over hips that practically didn't exist at all. There was something so pleasurable about touching Jeremy all over—something she had never felt before. Even years ago, her husband, Brad, out of the Marines, had never felt like Jeremy. Jean continued her game, slowly, slowly, moving down Jeremy's body, still keeping her eyes closed. With her eyes shut, Jeremy somehow seemed more real—Why?

Maybe seeing him—so handsome and so young—reminded her of who she really was. Not Jeremy's young girlfriend but one of his middle-aged clients. It was also the mirrors. If her eyes were open she'd be forced to watch every moment of their lovemaking endlessly reflected in the walls of the workout room. The thought of seeing herself screwing on an exercise mat in the shadow of a Nautilus machine made her blush. It also made her feel guilty—but not guilty enough to stop.

For years, guilt had kept her from even acknowledging how lonely she felt. After all, she had everything. Hard-

working husband, successful children, money. It was as if
she didn't have a right to feel something was missing—
especially because it was difficult to label her discontent,
to put it neatly into words. But if words didn't come easily,
images did. She had only to recall last night, when the
weekend was drawing to an end, to be reminded of the
empty feelings, the restlessness. Jean had undressed. As
usual Brad was already in bed reading: *Barron's*, *Business
Week*, *The Economist* were piled evenly on his nightstand.
He looked, Jean thought, as neat in bed as he did out of it:
his pinstriped suit replaced by Brooks Brothers pajamas.
Before she even got into bed Jean knew what would happen. When Brad finished the article, he'd turn to Jean for
sex. He'd make sure she had an orgasm, come himself,
kiss her goodnight, and roll over to sleep. It rarely varied.
Jean thought wryly, "The most novel thing Brad ever does
in bed is to change from long-sleeved pj's to short-sleeved
ones every April."

But last night had been a bit different. Brad had noticed
Jean for once. "Jean, you drank an awful lot of wine at
dinner at the club today. By the time I came off the ninth
hole you couldn't hit a tennis ball back over the net. You
really ought to watch it."

"Don't tell me how to run my life," Jean muttered back.
"Anyway, I didn't know you were so concerned with pro-
priety. Next thing I know, you won't allow me to play with
the pro—what with his reputation."

As Jean let the words go, she regretted it. Brad was a
good man—he never hurt her intentionally—why did she
need to strike out at him. Opening her mouth to apologize,
Jean looked at Brad and found she couldn't speak. He
looked so damned self-righteous; he was too used to hearing "Yes, darling," from her. Brad was clearly indignant
over her back talk but considered the notion of her threatened impropriety with the pro to be absurd. The thought—
let alone the action—was untenable to him.

He ignored her comments. If he was hurt, it didn't
show—nothing ever did—and in a moment he recovered.
"Now that Elliot's off to college I think you're bored.
That's why you're running off to a pottery class before you

even finish that exercise program. You need to get seriously involved in something. How much time can you spend shopping, anyway? Stuart's wife, Sandra, runs the United Way Campaign—why don't you give her a call. You have too much time on your hands; that's the trouble."

Jean loved Brad's "perfect" solutions to their problems. It was always someone—other than Brad, of course—who would include Jean. He never offered himself. How could he; there was "his work." Brad's work was his own separate world. Only when he needed her as his hostess was she ever included, though included was hardly the way she felt. She knew Brad's sermon would continue. But through the years she had grown expert at tuning him out. Only his last words really stuck: "Sometimes, Jean, I just don't understand you."

Even now with Jeremy beside her, those words echoed in her head. She looked at Jeremy realizing that he, unlike Brad, listened. And more than anything else she valued that. Understand? Yes, that was the problem in her marriage: somewhere each of them had ceased to understand.

DISCERNING THE PATTERN OF CONFLICT

As with most things in life, Brad is firm regarding his wish: "At the end of a hard day, I have to come home to a good woman. If I don't have that, I don't have a marriage, as far as I'm concerned."

Jean has her own longing. "I want to be married. But my vision of marriage is not two ships passing in the night. I want my marriage to be two people really involved with each other, caring for each other."

What they actually have is something altogether different. Brad has a mounting impatience with his wife, and Jean has a growing well of loneliness that has already prompted her to search for something or someone to fill the gap. Jean seems near the breaking point—as if one more word from Brad will cause her to unload the full extent of her misery. Brad's position may seem less extreme, but were he to discover Jean's affair he too would move beyond his breaking point. This marriage, though of long duration, is extremely vulnerable. It seems only a matter of time before the relationship may rupture, perhaps irreversibly. But Jean and Brad can pull back from the brink—by understanding the needs behind their conflict.

Jean is a woman with a need to fill an emotional vacuum, to find meaning in her life. There is a unique quality to Jean's need: for the first fifteen years of her marriage *it did not emerge*. Lying dormant, her need did not create conflict or threaten her marriage. For many years the empty space inside was filled up. Jean was engaged in the activities, concerns, and responsibilities of a mother and wife. This allowed her to feel satisfied and fulfilled. Only now, with her children grown and independent, with the role of wife and mother no longer new, fresh, and exciting, does a sense of emptiness and aloneness emerge. Only now that it is just the two of them does she turn to Brad with the full force of her emotional longing—and she finds him unsatisfying.

And Brad, the man to whom she turns—what is his unconscious need? Pervading his life and therefore his marriage is his need to remain detached from his emotions. He unconsciously believes that to display feeling, to be emotionally responsive, is to admit weakness. At all costs he must demonstrate to the world—and to himself—that nothing gets to him. He must stay cool, contained, self-possessed, undisturbed emotionally.

It's no wonder this marriage is so vulnerable. It isn't just Jean's affairs and her drinking. It isn't just Brad's work or his neglect of her. Jean is a woman who has grown to need more emotionally, and Brad is—as he has always been—a man closed off, a man unable to give. In fact, Brad's need makes him feel threatened by Jean's new and powerful emotional demands.

Theirs is a marriage that has become *emotionally* out of sync. Uncovering their very different needs offers the only chance for making this marriage work, for making them once again two people in harmony.

IS YOUR HUSBAND LIKE BRAD?

Brad may be someone who sounds all too familiar—too cool, too collected, with an aloofness that heightens your aloneness. You may be feeling the frustration of marriage to a man who buttons down his emotions along with his collars. Think about the things that upset you and you may unearth his need to keep emotionally detached.

Your complaint:
"He never gets mad. He's always the rational one. Somehow when things go wrong, only I'm bothered. It's infuriating."

Your husband's need:
Leading with the head and never the heart indicates his need at work.

Your complaint:
"When it comes to sex he has no imagination. We never experiment or really go wild."

Your husband's need:
Passion means letting go. To prevent the show of such intense feelings, he transforms what has the potential for pleasure into a routine.

Your complaint:
"He accuses me of being too emotional, or too outspoken, or too sensitive, or too sentimental. . . ."

Your husband's need:
Convincing himself that displays of emotion are wrong helps make his restraint feel right.

Your complaint:
"He'd notice if dinner were late but I don't think he knows how bad things are with me, with us. Or at least he never acknowledges it."

Your husband's need:
When outside interferences are disruptive, he notices. But he doesn't allow the same attention to be turned inward. Scrutinizing the outside world may help divert him from the inner world of feelings he is reluctant to acknowledge.

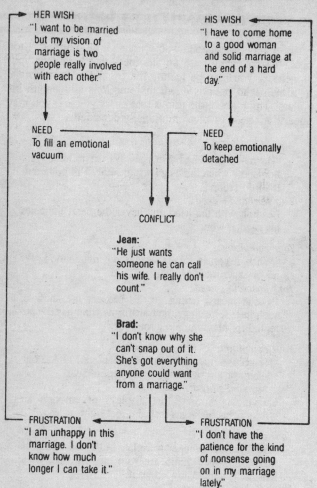

HER WISH
"I want to be married but my vision of marriage is two people really involved with each other."

HIS WISH
"I have to come home to a good woman and solid marriage at the end of a hard day."

NEED
To fill an emotional vacuum

NEED
To keep emotionally detached

CONFLICT

Jean:
"He just wants someone he can call his wife. I really don't count."

Brad:
"I don't know why she can't snap out of it. She's got everything anyone could want from a marriage."

FRUSTRATION
"I am unhappy in this marriage. I don't know how much longer I can take it."

FRUSTRATION
"I don't have the patience for the kind of nonsense going on in my marriage lately."

Your complaint:
   "He's a cold fish."
Your husband's need:
   Hot blood comes from connecting with intense feel-

ings. A detached man sacrifices the pleasure of true passion and intimacy on the altar of restraint.

Your husband's shortcomings may seem noticeable as well in his relations with your children. Perhaps he turns off to them, especially when they're distressed. With his need, the display of emotion in others, particularly in those so close, is too threatening. He turns off to the children (and to you) because he must turn off to himself.

You may also be irritated with your husband's priorities. To your dismay, work, church, politics, and so forth may be at the center of his life—not you. Devotion to a cause is the single best way a man can steer clear of his personal emotions. By filling up his life with pursuits, he never has to stop and admit how vital you are to him, how much someone he loves means to him. As a result, you feel he's made you unimportant.

The kind of social network you've had to develop may also irk you. Perhaps you feel dragged through a set of predictable rituals (dinner parties, corporate luncheons, charity balls). You conclude with irritation, "We're never alone." Your social calendar may be filled with events but devoid of meaning. Your husband is using activities, as well as other people, to help keep things light, unserious, superficial—on a level where he feels safe and strong—a kind of safety in numbers. Most probably your cool, calm, and unresponsive man is not as strong as he wants the world and himself to believe.

Bear in mind that if your man never asks you what you care about, or how you truly feel, these may well be the very questions he does not ask himself. If the man in your life—like Brad—loves you but is unable to show it, he may well be displaying a need to preserve emotional detachment.

ARE YOU LIKE JEAN?

Your Need:

Perhaps a restless discontent has been stirring within your life as it has within Jean's. It may be your need to fill an emotional vacuum that is the source of the nagging feeling that life should be something more. Analyzing the complaints of your spouse will help unlock this truth about yourself.

> *Your husband's complaint:*
> "She eats nonstop. She's out shopping every day. Our phone bills are enormous. She reads one romance novel after another."
>
> *Your need:*
> If you are compulsively filling up your body, your time, or your mind, you may actually be trying to stop a feeling of emptiness from consuming you.

> *Your husband's complaint:*
> "She's got everything she wants and needs, but she's unhappy. And what's more, she doesn't even know why."
>
> *Your need:*
> The material things you have do not confer inner meaning. This may confuse your husband, and you, but self-worth just can't be determined by a person's net worth.

> *Your husband's complaint:*
> "She's gone from aerobics class, to tennis, to night classes. Nothing holds her interest. She doesn't take anything seriously."
>
> *Your need:*
> In each pursuit, you unconsciously seek something to make you feel better inside. Each interest fails to do that, so you move on. Your need can drive you from one activity to another in search of fulfillment: hence your apparent lack of commitment.

Your husband's complaint:
   "I am the same man she married, only now she tells
   me I seem distant, like a stranger."
Your need:
   In the first blush of marriage and family, excitement,
   novelty, even struggle filled up your life. Whatever
   he gave, no matter how little, was enough. Now that
   it's just the two of you, you may feel pain as you
   discover how little emotional exchange there actually
   is between you. You feel the longing now that you
   couldn't feel then.

Your husband's complaint:
   "She's been drinking too much."
Your need:
   Alcohol numbs. You may be attempting to silence
   the feelings aroused by your need.

   Your need may compel you to behavior that would provoke powerful complaints in your husband—if he knew
everything about you. Sensing just how disruptive this
knowledge could be, you keep it under wraps. You yourself may feel your behavior is wrong. For instance, you
may be seeing other men or carrying on a full-blown affair.
If you are involved in extramarital connections (especially
if they are thrilling but brief), it may be the excitement
you're really after: that rush of excitement can act as a
distraction from inner turmoil. Sex is only one form of
distraction. Gambling and drugs are others. Like sex, they
may also be your secret. Ironically, your husband is un-
likely to discover these secrets. His emotional detachment
keeps him from putting two and two together. He denies
the undeniable.
   Fortunately your relationship can be lifted off the pre-
carious course on which it is running. Uncovering each
other's needs can bring you together and help each of you
to begin to understand.

BRAD'S PAST

Brad has an early and vivid memory of his parents. "I must have been four or five. I'd been sent to bed in the usual way—I went downstairs to kiss my parents' cheeks and then was tucked into bed by our housekeeper. But I knew something was going on, so one time after Elsa had closed the door I snuck out of bed and down the hall to the top of the staircase. At the foot of the stairs were my parents. They must have been going to a charity ball; they were always doing that sort of thing. To me they looked like a king and queen—my mother was wearing a beautiful gown. I sat staring and didn't say a word. They went off and I stayed there. Apparently I fell asleep. I woke up and it was dark. I was scared and I cried. My parents were still out. Elsa, downstairs asleep, didn't hear me at first. I don't know how long it took, but Elsa finally came and put me to bed. In her German accent she told me, 'Ve von't tell your mamma and pappa and spoil their goot time.'" Brad kept the promise. Brad's parents did hear what had happened but from Elsa, who assured them that he had gone to bed like a "little man." The label "our little man" stuck, and Brad remembers wearing it proudly.

"My parents weren't coddlers. They didn't put much store in crying. They both had a particular view about how to raise children—a certain sense of correctness. That's the way we were treated: correctly. We carried on a family tradition. When Papa Adolf, my father's father, was still alive, I can remember him complimenting my mother that her children were just the way they should be: 'Seen but not heard.'

"My parents are very close; they rarely do things apart. But they're not especially demonstrative people—I never saw them kiss or hug in front of us. They're reserved with us too. To this day if my brother, Todd, or I bring home good news, my father shakes our hands. Todd can't always take my father's style. But Todd needs to toughen up. They had to send him to three boarding schools before he found one he could make it through."

What Brad remembers most is the way his parents gave him his sense of self-reliance. Whether it was tying shoelaces at four or sailing at nine, his parents showed him once, and that was enough. As Brad recalls, "Not only was once enough, but I took pleasure in being able to do things on my own. That's a good part of the reason I asked to go to Hotchkiss Academy. I looked forward to being self-reliant. My parents were all for it. They knew Hotchkiss' reputation for building character.

"When I look back I think it's my upbringing that allowed me to do so well in college and in the military and now at work. Look, I'm proud that I can handle situations, that I'm not weak. I don't come undone, as so many people seem to these days."

Brad's parents' correctness and civility were a cover for their coldness. Involved with each other and devoted to their own pursuits, pleasures, and concerns, they weren't very involved with their children. They were interested in their children only as extensions of themselves—as family members who would add to the honor of the family name, who would preserve what was all-important to them: the family image.

A devotion to developing nondemanding, nonemotional, self-reliant children was really their way of raising kids with whom they didn't have to bother. They couldn't give, so they created a value system where asking was considered inappropriate—a sign of weakness. With Brad they succeeded. He has incorporated their belief system; he carries on their "tradition." But he fails to appreciate that this is the way he survived their emotional indifference—by identifying with them. In being like them, he avoided the pain of their aloofness. He was, as the image of him on the staircase so poignantly conveys, a lonely little boy who made those feelings go away by becoming the brave "little man." This was something his brother just couldn't do. Being a "little man" protected Brad, but at a great sacrifice: it cut him off from his inner feelings. He learned to be restrained and correct but didn't develop his capacity for warmth, love, and intimate contact. As an adult he remains very much the same. He copes successfully but at the price of losing sight of his inner life.

IS THIS YOUR HUSBAND'S PAST?

Is your self-assured, self-reliant husband a man who is determined to remain detached from his feelings?

His parents were advocates of self-reliance, willpower, perseverance.
> *Noble qualities sometimes serve selfish purposes. This may well have been his family's recipe for ensuring "one batch of trouble-free kids."*

He idealizes, praises, and copies his parents' child-rearing methods—even though they were stern, austere, even harsh.
> *A child who suffers sometimes manages to dispel the pain by becoming like his parents, adopting and embracing their values, attitudes, style. Unconsciously he feels to join 'em is to lick 'em.*

He was a competent, accomplished boy. He caught on to things quickly.
> *Some children adapt to uninvolved parents by precocious self-reliance. They learn to take care of themselves early, so as not to risk counting on Mom and Dad to come through. Your husband became competent but he couldn't possibly provide for himself what parents alone can give—emotional nurturance and caring. What your husband didn't get, he can't give. As an adult he remains good at everything but caring.*

Look at the expressions families use to label children. They often reveal what is valued and what is not; what is accepted, what is spurned. For Brad's family, children fell into two categories: "little men" and "cry babies." Did your husband's parents also convey to their children the message that children are appealing as long as they keep up appearances, as long as they reveal no inner moods, no unpleasant feelings? If so, no wonder your husband short-circuits connections to and from his inner domain.

In Brad's family, his brother, Todd, was considered weak. Some parents fault a child rather than question themselves. Such dismissal may be part of your husband's family history. He continues to behave toward himself in the same way—ignoring and dismissing his own complex emotions.

Perhaps your husband, like Brad, survived aloof and uninterested parents by disconnecting emotionally. But his feelings are there—somewhere—waiting to be tapped. They aren't absent or nonexistent; they are locked away for safekeeping. They are somewhere to be found. Your husband is capable of giving, once he gets to his own insides.

JEAN'S PAST

"Do you remember that old coffee commercial? The peasants of Colombia standing around waiting for 'El Exigente' to give the thumbs up or down on their coffee crop. The air is filled with hushed anticipation—you can cut the silence with a knife. Then His Excellency gives his okay —suddenly the silence breaks and every peasant is dancing with joy. That's my father and our family. I think the world of my father. He wasn't mean or a tyrant—actually he could be very nice—but he was definitely 'El Exigente.' His home was his castle. What we did, what we thought, what we bought, where we went were his decisions. I remember for years Mother wanted air-conditioning in our car, but my father decided it wasn't necessary. Result: we didn't get it. Then a few years later, he wanted it. Result: we got it. Everything was like that. Even his moods determined how we all felt. You could see it on my mother's face. If she walked around the house humming and smiling, it meant my father was feeling good. A martini in her hand was a sure sign Dad had had a bad day. Emotionally, Mom was his Siamese twin. She lived through him. He wasn't ever cruel, but all our lives—my mother's, mine, and my three sisters'—had to revolve around his.

"He was quite successful professionally; he was with a big chemical firm. His corporate headquarters relocated, and in order for Dad to get a promotion he wanted, we had to move west. It was just before my sixth grade graduation. I pleaded with my mother to let me stay with our neighbors just till the graduation and prom were over. My father decided a sixth grade graduation and prom were ridiculous and unimportant and nothing to change plans over. My mother, as always, went along with him. She broke the news to me with 'Don't upset Daddy; it's for the best.' We moved six weeks before the prom. I felt so hurt and lost, it was unbelievable. In my own room I cried a lot. But not in front of my father. The strange thing was that my father was so pleased about moving that the minute I got on the plane I forgot about being miserable. Listening to my dad talk about our new house, the pool, and maybe a pony had us all excited. It was as if the plane trip was a ride on a magic carpet. My dad could do that—infect us with his enthusiasm.

"I never regretted moving. The kids were a lot better than the ones in my hometown. In fact, I ended up getting in with a good crowd and being pretty popular. My clique stayed together right through high school. Almost all the girls became cheerleaders and the guys ended up on either the basketball or football teams. For a while I even went steady with the basketball team captain.

"On Saturday nights there was always a party to go to at someone's house, and on Monday mornings, my best friend, Kathy, and I would pass notes back and forth about everything we did over the weekend. We were totally boy-crazy in high school. It's no wonder I just pulled by with a C in history. But actually I was never that interested in studying. I did okay, but school was just something to get through. I think that may be why I didn't mind staying home and going to college locally while Brad went away to college. (We met the summer before his junior year when I had just finished high school.) At the end of my sophomore year, I dropped out of college and married Brad. It was what I had always wanted—to get married and have a family.

"I remember that hole-in-the-wall apartment we first had. I really devoted myself to making it a cozy home and Brad really worked hard getting himself launched on a career. In some ways those were the best years."

Jean is aware that in her family, life centered on her father—mother and daughters were the satellites whirling in orbit around him. But Jean is unaware of the subtle and powerful message her mother's lack of independence conveyed: a woman derives her meaning in life from attachment to a man. Without it she risks feeling insignificant or meaningless. From her mother, Jean learned that a man, not a woman, has what counts. This became Jean's unconscious view of herself. On her own, she feels a lack of self-regard, self-importance, a kind of emptiness.

For most of her life Jean succeeded in filling the gap—with first her father, then boyfriends, then Brad, and later children. Through these attachments, she gained a sense of completion, well-being, and purpose. Jean's need to fill an emotional vacuum has always been there but she has always filled it. Now her need, which lay dormant all these years, has emerged to give rise to marital conflict.

Jean is a woman who has gained meaning in her life through others. Now, as a mature woman, wishing to be heard and understood, she has unconsciously set out in search of her *own* special value. Understanding the need that drives this quest can help Jean find herself without losing her marriage.

IS THIS YOUR PAST?

Are you, like Jean, seeking meaning in your life, searching at last for emotional fulfillment?

Your family lived in the shadow of your father. You were Daddy's girl.
> *Living with a man who never stops seeming larger than life can leave a girl feeling inadequate. Only a man gets a place in the sun.*

Your mother was wrapped up in your father and easily influenced by him.

A mother who seems profoundly affected by a man may convey the message, "Without him I'm a nobody." This may become the belief you have about yourself.

As a teenager you were boy-crazy and very popular; you ignored your own education and goals. You quit school (or never went at all) when you married.

Being "too busy" for school and ignoring your personal growth may signal your lack of belief that you have what it takes. Your sense of fulfillment had to come from the outside.

Jean's past is not filled with unpleasant memories. You, too, may feel that your past was not unhappy. But sometimes, conflicts arise out of too much of what may seem like a good thing. If you were a daddy's girl who idealized and cherished your father, your own needs and self-worth may not have been attended to. This emotional one-way street may leave you feeling empty inside, may leave you convinced that on your own you just don't count.

Perhaps you too grew in the shadow of your father. Now you are seeking some time in the sun.

LINDA and MARC:
The Wicked Stepmother

Eight-year-old Jonathan silently picked at his plate of now-cold spaghetti. His ten-year-old brother, Cary, sat pouting, not even bothering to sample dinner. "The only reason we get stuck with spaghetti is because Lauren loves it," Cary whined, pointing at his stepsister who sat smiling in her high chair, covered with tomato sauce and singularly oblivious to the mounting tension. "And Dad says you should make us something *we* like," piped in Jonathan. With Marc sitting at the table just waiting to see her reaction, Linda felt ready to bolt. Cary and Jonathan were impossibly spoiled and it was Marc's fault. Ever since they'd married, he'd been overindulging his boys. The few times Linda raised an objection, pointing out how differently Marc treated their daughter, Lauren, he defended himself with one sharp retort, "Her parents aren't divorced—yet!" The topic was closed.

Initially, Linda had swallowed her anger and let the issue slide—after all, the boys came only every other weekend and holidays. But now circumstances had changed radically. At thirty-four, Marc's ex-wife, Barbara, had decided to start medical school. Now in her third year, Barbara claimed she couldn't manage the boys *and* school and had turned them over to Marc. Every other weekend was now reserved for Barbara, instead of Marc.

Linda could understand Marc's delight at the change; he had initially fought for joint custody. But Linda, who hadn't wanted to have children right away, had found herself pregnant with Lauren only a year after the wedding and was less than overjoyed at her two new arrivals.

Only by reassuring herself that the arrangement wasn't permanent could Linda hang on to her sanity. Whatever the boys wanted, they got. The guest room was redone entirely to their specifications. And they *had* to have a computer—though they already had one at their mother's—which was bought with the money Linda and Marc had earlier planned to spend on a new color TV. Marc could easily say no to Linda, but when it came to Cary and Jonathan, the word didn't exist.

Linda and Marc had no privacy anymore, and their sex life had suffered. Several nights a week Jonathan's nightmares wakened him. He would come into their room clutching his Pillow Person and Marc never objected to his curling up in a sleeping bag on their bedroom floor. Linda knew Jonathan needed help, but she also knew that this kind of arrangement was no solution. One night when she had suggested that he ought to go back to his own room, she had heard Marc mutter under his breath, "Selfish bitch."

Unfortunately, having the boys full-time did little to alter Marc's attitude. Even now, instead of telling his boys to eat their supper, Marc probably expected Linda to smile and ask them what they would prefer instead. Linda felt trapped in a no-win situation. If she cooked something else, she'd be angry with herself and furious at Marc and the boys. If she didn't, they'd all be irritated with her. She waited for her husband to make the first move.

Though silent, Marc wasn't oblivious to the goings-on. Seeing her eyebrows arched, her lips pursed, he was sure it was Linda's disdain for the boys coming through. Angrily Marc mused to himself, "It wouldn't hurt her if she tried harder for them and maybe did something more than just open a can. When we were first married and it was just the two of us, Linda couldn't do enough."

Now, even special times together were a series of disasters. He remembered last Christmas: to make everyone happy, he had ferried the boys around from his ex-wife's to his ex-in-laws', to his parents' and finally home. He had known he'd be late, but Linda would just have to understand. He had come home to find Linda in tears. "Can't your ex-wife share the burden? What about your parents? Why does it always have to be you, and you alone? Don't you think Lauren and I deserve Christmas with you too?" It had been a miserable holiday for everyone.

Now looking at Linda, Marc was at a loss. She was pulling him apart when what he needed was her help. Linda, too, felt unhappy, looking at two lovable little boys who were complicating her life and the man she loved who was making her miserable. Suddenly a bowl of spaghetti was a very big issue.

DISCERNING THE PATTERN OF CONFLICT

Is the real source of trouble for Marc and Linda the spaghetti for dinner, the extra computer, the spoiled kids, the wicked stepmother, or the ex-wife? These are *stresses* on the relationship but they are not the actual roots of the conflict. The true conflict is between two people's unconscious needs. Unrecognized and unresolved, these needs are the source of frustration; they create the gulf between what you want from your marriage and what you feel you get.

Let's look more carefully at Marc and Linda. Marc's wish is to have a neat, smooth, well-oiled relationship: "I thought Linda was so cheerful and caring that we'd make it work." Yet for the second time in his life, a happy family —the model of respectability and solidity that's so much a part of his upbringing—seems out of his grasp. Marc is aware that he has failed to achieve his wish, but he does not understand the unconscious need that lies at the root of his disappointment. Marc's need is to be perfect, to be in control. With this need, anything that goes wrong in his marriage, any dissatisfaction or complaint, makes him un-

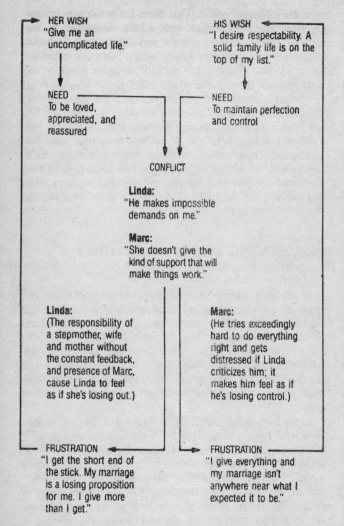

HER WISH
"Give me an uncomplicated life."

HIS WISH
"I desire respectability. A solid family life is on the top of my list."

NEED
To be loved, appreciated, and reassured

NEED
To maintain perfection and control

CONFLICT

Linda:
"He makes impossible demands on me."

Marc:
"She doesn't give the kind of support that will make things work."

Linda:
(The responsibility of a stepmother, wife and mother without the constant feedback, and presence of Marc, cause Linda to feel as if she's losing out.)

Marc:
(He tries exceedingly hard to do everything right and gets distressed if Linda criticizes him; it makes him feel as if he's losing control.)

FRUSTRATION
"I get the short end of the stick. My marriage is a losing proposition for me. I give more than I get."

FRUSTRATION
"I give everything and my marriage isn't anywhere near what I expected it to be."

comfortable. Because of his unrecognized demand that his world be ideal, he quickly feels irritation when things are not as they "ought" to be. This drive for perfection brings him into repeated conflict with Linda. Unaware of his need, he feels, "I don't get the kind of support to make things work. All I get is complaints." Marc thinks the problem is that Linda doesn't fulfill his wish for a happy family, but the problem is his need at work.

What are the wish and the need that Linda brings to the relationship? Linda can easily describe her wish. "With Marc I was really expecting a warm family life—I thought I could depend on him. I know any relationship will have problems, but I thought that with his kind of strength, we'd have as few as possible." Linda's wish for a relatively uncomplicated relationship does not seem excessive, but Linda is unaware of the need that surrounds this longing. Linda is insecure. She has a need for complete attention and caring, a need to be reassured. Her sense that Marc is not totally hers disturbs, even frightens her. Without reassurance that she is loved, responsibilities, demands, and compromises make Linda feel that she's losing out. Ironically, when she is asked to share and to give, she feels as if something is being taken away. When Linda cries, "Everybody wants something from me," her need is creating her frustration.

Think of Linda and the complaints Marc has: her reluctance to cook, her unwillingness to indulge the boys, her insistence on spending the holiday with Marc. The common theme is sharing, giving, doing for others—areas that make Linda feel uncomfortable, hurt, threatened, or deprived. All of which suggest a need to be totally loved and appreciated. And Marc? To Linda, he seems demanding, brooks no criticism about the boys, expects Sunday night dinners to be banquets, and gets angry at her demands on his time. Marc feels strain when all doesn't go smoothly. A need to be in control gives common meaning to the various complaints. Without insight into the needs that create their pattern, the conflict will spin on and on.

IS YOUR HUSBAND LIKE MARC?

If the man in your life has an unconscious need to control, these are the sorts of complaints you might be expressing. As you begin to understand his need, which is the source of your complaints, you'll be able to tackle the true conflicts of your relationship.

Your complaint:

"He works too much; he doesn't know how to relax. He prides himself on giving his all, on being excellent—but he doesn't know how to do it any other way."

Your husband's need:

Being excellent is his way of staying on top of things. He is unable to ease up on the strict expectations he has for himself.

Your complaint:

"If things aren't just so, he acts like it's the end of the world. He can't understand that with a home and kids—unlike his work—things are bound to get out of hand sometimes."

Your husband's need:

Unfinished business bothers him—a lack of completion feels like disorder. With his need, order, completion, and perfection are priorities.

Your complaint:

"I want to meet him halfway; he wants to be the boss. He treats me like I'm one of the kids."

Your husband's need:

Having power is having control, which assures that things go his way—the only way.

Your complaint:

"He never wants to hear what's really bothering me. Sometimes I think it annoys him to face the fact that we're having troubles."

Your husband's need:

Having troubles is an admission that he's not perfect, which is something he's not able to acknowledge.

Your complaint:
"He'd like to forget about his first marriage. He wants us to be one big happy stepfamily."

Your husband's need:
Acting as if the past never happened helps him feel that he can erase his mistakes—the moments when he couldn't control his world. His need forces him into rewriting history to erase failures.

Linda complains, "I can never question Marc about anything; he clams up. It's as if I put a knife through his heart." Perhaps your husband also is uncomfortable being questioned. Or perhaps you feel, "He can't stand any disagreement. He wants a woman who will yes him to death. I don't open my mouth anymore—he just walks away if I do." A man with a need to be perfect views any questions, any disagreement, as personal criticism. He feels personally assaulted; therefore, he finds it intolerable to work on problems.

Does your man always have to be right? Does he always have to have the last word? If he seems self-righteous to you, he's demonstrating his need to be in control. Do you complain that he's stiff, inflexible, uptight, or too serious? You may find him fussy; you may resent that he always expects everything to be just so. He's inflexible because he's uncomfortable with the unpredictable. His need keeps him from letting go. Having everything perfect supports his feeling that life is entirely under control.

Perhaps you feel that you can't be yourself when you're with your husband—that he's overly concerned with being respected and oversensitive to anything you may do in public. Your man may be worried about his image and anything or anyone that might reflect it. Like everything else he's got to keep his image under his own control. He can't leave anything to chance. This creates impossible standards for you and him.

ARE YOU LIKE LINDA?

Now give yourself the opportunity to see whether you, like Linda, have a need to feel completely cared for. Your insecurities may leave you open to disappointment, which creates conflict with your man.

Your husband's complaint:
"Anger is always simmering under her skin. No matter what I do, I'm in the hole with her."
Your need:
Because your need makes you insecure about your man's love and supersensitive to everything he does or doesn't do, you are vulnerable to hurt and disappointment. Disappointed people often behave angrily.

Your husband's complaint:
"She's so lazy. She never extends herself; she never makes the extra effort for anyone I care about."
Your need:
When you yourself feel deprived, you find having to provide for others overwhelming, paralyzing—any effort is too much.

Your husband's complaint:
"It takes a long time to turn her on. I'm not sure she's really interested in sex—she'd rather cuddle than fuck."
Your need:
Lack of interest is not the problem. You're very sexual, but you need tenderness, you need to feel cared for, in order to be relaxed and comfortable having sex.

Your husband's complaint:
"She's so hard to satisfy—she never has enough. She doesn't know what she wants."
Your need:
What you want emotionally is to be totally understood—an expectation difficult for anyone to satisfy. This leaves you and your man feeling frustrated and impotent.

Your husband's complaint:

"If it were up to her, my kids would fit into our lives Sunday from one to four, period. What does she expect from a man with kids of his own? Should I cut them out of my life?"

Your need:

Your need for total involvement blinds you to your man's commitment to others. You deny their importance, unconsciously hoping he will too. Your need makes you feel that others—even children—are your competitors.

Marc feels that Linda is selfish: "It's as if any request on her time is an imposition." If you seem selfish to your husband, it is because you are struggling to hold on to what you have. Your need makes you feel that to give may be the same as to lose.

Your need often leaves you feeling deprived. Your husband may find that though he knows you like sex, you just can't seem to get into it: "We have great sex—provided we're alone and a hundred miles from home." Feeling so deprived during your days, you can't easily let go of this feeling in bed. On vacation, for example, when you have your husband's complete attention, you free yourself of this sense of deprivation.

Does your husband complain that you're very jealous? Because you crave caring, it's hard for you to believe your man loves you when his attention is diverted from you—even momentarily. Perhaps he feels that you resent the time he gives to the kids, or his work, or his parents, and so on. Does he say, "If I don't include her, she gets mad, but not everything I do should involve her." It's hard for you not to personalize your man's actions. His interest in anyone else makes you feel as if he has no interest in you.

MARC'S PAST

Marc grew up in Houston. Though he attended college out of state, neither he nor anyone in his family doubted that he'd return. It was a given that he, like his father, would take over the family haberdashery business. Marc was hardly the kind of person who'd think of breaking tradition.

This sense of responsibility was nothing new. Even as a small boy, Marc had been serious—giving his all to anything he attempted. "Mother often told the story of how I learned to ride my bike. I disappeared one morning with my two-wheeler and came back three hours later black-and-blue but knowing how to ride. 'Just like you,' she'd say, 'not to give up.'"

Marc's father was more critical. He not only expected the best from Marc; he demanded it. "If I brought a grade of 95 home, my father would ask, 'What happened to the other five points?' It sounds silly but everytime I took a test, the points that were missing became my focus." Even praise became a form of pressure. "My younger brother Jack was always hearing about my football records. I liked being special but I never felt free—just to let go, maybe make my own mistakes."

In high school and college, Marc dated only the "right" girls—pretty, intelligent, popular. "My college roommate ribbed me about women, 'Always five feet nine and under—that way Marc makes sure they're looking up at him.'"

His first wife, Barbara, intelligent and lively, did indeed look up to Marc. Everything from their June wedding to their suburban house and two children went according to plan—his plan.

Five years later Marc's marriage looked less than ideal. Absorbed in work, he became a Sunday husband and father. Oblivious to the impact of his neglect, it was only one night when he lost his erection while making love that he began to panic. Barbara was cold and uninterested, turning away, almost pleased at his impotence. A week later Barbara admitted to having a lover.

For Marc his marriage was over; he knew he'd never touch her again. Burning with righteous indignation, Marc dictated the terms of the divorce. No custody fight as long as Barbara made clear the split was her fault, her doing—a perfect husband with an imperfect wife.

Linda was an important step in getting Marc's life back

in order. Young, impressionable, and adoring, she offered a fresh start. Their lavish wedding epitomized this new beginning. Even Marc's mother commented, "The only way I knew it was a second wedding was seeing Jonathan and Cary coming down the aisle." Linda would help make everything right again.

What does Marc's life story reveal about his need?

Marc is a man laboring under an enormous burden: perfection. From an early age he learned that being loved was contingent on performing, doing well, living up to expectations. If he did well, he pleased his mother. His father's message was "I expect the best from you, but you never quite make it."

This attitude kept Marc in constant tension chasing after an unattainable perfection. The only way to cope with this pressure was by keeping things under control—setting standards and making sure they were met. Only by having things go smoothly and predictably can Marc feel a sense of mastery. That's why Marc "replaced" Barbara with Linda—he finds it too threatening to be in a relationship that's out of his control.

But Marc is not simply a child of demanding parents. By now, their demands have become his values, his standards—the forces that rule his emotional life.

IS THIS YOUR HUSBAND'S PAST?

Could your husband be the product of a past like Marc's? Many aspects of the way he was brought up may have contributed to his need to be perfect, his need to control.

His family had standards, pride.
He may have internalized that sense of pride, feeling as if his role in life is to be the standard bearer.

Ever since his first date, it's been important to him that he be seen with the right girl, that he bring home a pretty woman.
He grew up seeking public approval as a kind of

reassurance. Having the right person on his arm was his way of declaring, "All's right with my world."

He was the kind of child who'd give the bigger piece of cake to his sibling.

Being responsible, fair, and correct from an early age was his way of striving to be perfect.

Marc was much admired by his mother. If your husband was his mother's boy, her admiration carried with it expectations: "I'm depending on you; don't let me down." Your husband's father, on the other hand, may have been critical or silently demanding. A father who set goals and then makes the child feel he can never attain these goals sets in motion a man's endless chase of unrealizable perfection.

As a child, your husband had heroes—men he admired and wanted to be like. Even from a young age, perfection was your husband's pursuit, and these idols are perfect. Being a good student, a good athlete, and so forth was always important to your man. His quest for perfection easily transferred to any area he pursued.

Your husband's parents were proud of his tenacity, of the fact that he'd go it alone. He set up obstacles, challenges, tests—and made sure to overcome them on his own. Having to prove himself by himself was and is his way of maintaining a feeling of mastery.

LINDA'S PAST

As with Marc, Linda's need was established early on. Linda was her family's golden girl. Her parents and grandparents delighted in her good nature, her ever-present smile. Unlike her older brother Jason, she could always be counted on to give her parents pleasure. "You're as pretty as you are good," her father would comment.

Even as a teenager, Linda never caused her parents grief. While not a scholar, she was always teacher's pet and popular with friends. "My parents never pushed for A's. When I brought my report card, they'd give it a quick glance, nod, say, 'Fine,' and hand it back. They were more concerned with how I looked and acted. On Saturdays my father would stuff money into my mother's pocketbook and tell us to 'come back pretty.' He was very handsome and took a lot of pride in how he kept himself and us."

Though self-conscious about being flat-chested, Linda managed to make it through adolescence without acne or "the uglies." "My best years were high school. Sailing, cheerleading, dating. Nothing's ever really matched it."

Along with all her friends, Linda then went to college. Arizona State was just the right place for her—four or five dates a weekend. "I got so many calls that someone posted my room number on the phone. I never got serious with anyone, but I never felt there'd be any problem getting serious later."

Later for Linda turned out to be three years. Working as an assistant buyer for Neiman-Marcus, she met Marc while on an assignment to comparison shop his store. "Everything about him appealed to me. He was handsome, successful, so polished. Marc treated me with such respect. I was concerned about his being older and about the kids, but even my mother said, 'The way Marc handles things, I'm sure he won't let his past interfere with your life together.'"

Linda met Jonathan and Cary for the first time one Sunday. "After the zoo, Marc brought them and a pizza to my apartment. The boys pretty much ignored me. But I figured Marc would do things around town with them each Sunday, and one dinner a week is no great sacrifice."

By the time Linda said yes to Marc, she thought she had a notion of how things would be. "Actually the boys were a plus in one way: I wasn't eager to have children quickly and obviously Marc wouldn't pressure me. It could be the two of us until we were ready for a change."

How did this past give rise to Linda's need to be totally loved and appreciated? Having had no real demands put on her, Linda expects that if she is pleasing, if she is loving, those around her will respond—totally. Her parents, by adoring her, by treating her as a lovable plaything, created this unrealistic expectation of how the world would and should treat her. Ironically, it undermines her sense of self.

Only if she gets the right feedback does she feel reassured about her worth. She depends on a constant flow of attention and devotion to make her feel worthy. This serves to set her up for disappointment and pain. When total attention isn't given to her—and it often isn't—she feels things are terribly wrong. This is the root of her need: to be loved and appreciated.

IS THIS YOUR PAST?

Did your upbringing turn you into a woman like Linda? If you, too, are a woman who needs to be totally loved and appreciated, the following will strike a familiar chord.

Your parents never made demands on you. They cared but didn't apply pressure.

> *Parents who don't ask a child to compromise, to give, to reciprocate, may create a woman who is unable to make the compromises necessary to have a satisfying adult life.*

You were cute, adorable, the little star. You parents loved to show you off.

> *Ironically, your parents created a dependency in you on feedback and attention. This undermined your self-worth, leaving you feeling that it's your performance, not yourself that is loved. As a result, even today, you feel insecure about how lovable you are.*

At home, you didn't hear the word "no" much. You might not have been terribly demanding, but you always got what you wanted.

> *In order to maintain an adult partnership, you have to be able to tolerate frustration—an ability you never had a chance to develop.*

Were you like Linda the precious, lovable, favorite child? Then from an early age you were appreciated—with little effort on your part. The feeling that appreciation is due to you follows you into adulthood. As a child, you rarely evoked negative feelings from your parents. This taught you the emotional equation, "If I'm nice, everything goes smoothly." Never having had to do more than be yourself, you feel angry and confused when, as an adult, you find the formula no longer works.

You weren't a rebellious adolescent and were shocked by your friends' turbulent relationships with their parents. Since you were insulated from the frictions that are normal between parent and child, you never learned how to work frictions through.

Your parents never made an issue out of your achieving at school, in a career, and so forth. They assumed you'd end up married. This left you with a sense that everything will simply fall into place in life. As an adult, when things don't fall into place, you feel frustration, dissatisfaction.

PART THREE

Can Your Marriage Be Saved?

"I love Marc, and he loves me, but our fear is that if things don't change soon, love won't be enough to keep us together."

—Linda

If you feel the way Linda feels, you must be eager, at this point, to begin negotiating a better relationship. You've learned about the risks your marriage faces and you've developed insight into the true nature of your marital problems. But there's one more step that Linda and Marc had to deal with before negotiation could begin, and you must too. You need to demonstrate to yourself that you believe your marriage can be saved and is worth saving.

When your conflicts are at their worst, you probably find yourself thinking, "There's nothing left in this for me." Now is the time to challenge that preconceived notion, to decide that there is a hell of a lot more here for you, if you can get yourselves out from under. Most of us have an emotional investment in a marriage. Even in the most battered and strained of relationships, we continue to care. This, coupled with a hopeful vision—the belief that things can get better—makes change possible.

How can you gauge the resilience of your marriage? How can you know the strengths of your emotional bonds?

183

How can you tell if your marriage is negotiable? You can
find answers to these questions by uncovering the positive
feelings you have about your marriage. Sometimes, under
the weight of your unhappiness or burdened by your marital difficulties, you may lose sight of your positive feelings. They needn't elude you. By taking time, you can
draw out, and eventually draw upon, the reservoir of caring
feelings contained within you.

Thirteen questions follow—and on this occasion, thirteen may be your lucky number. These thirteen questions
will help you find those strengths, restore those positive
feelings. Think them through. Try not to hurry. Give yourself the chance to reflect on each.

Each question is followed by an explanation of the importance of the positive feeling the question seeks to uncover. Be sure to answer the question *before* you read the
explanation. These questions require you to look deeply
into your feelings. Think them through—before you go on
to the explanations. Do not expect to have positive answers
to all the questions. Your honest answers are the only ones
that can help you decide whether your marriage can be
saved.

Some of the explanations include the responses of the
gridlocked couples. We will be following Marc and Linda,
the last couple in the Marital Gridlock section, through this
section into the actual negotiation chapter that follows, and
you will see just how the negotiation techniques work. But
the answers of Marc and Linda and of the other couples are
simply examples. Your answers will be different—each
partnership has its own strengths, its own positive qualities
to draw upon.

UNCOVERING THE POSITIVE FEELINGS: THIRTEEN QUESTIONS

Can you conjure up a fantasy of how things could be
better—of how your marriage would work "if only
things were different"?

Remember to answer each question before you move on to the explanation.

If you can imagine satisfaction, bonds still exist between you and your husband. Reality may never become as good as you dream of it, but the fact that you can dream reflects your emotional connection. Wishful thinking can be a powerful emotional bond. If you can imagine that things can be better, they often can be.

Take Marc and Linda's responses, for example. Although Marc's need to have things perfect makes him unhappy with his marriage, it also makes him optimistic. "I can't stop thinking of a better future—my family's happiness." And Linda hasn't lost sight of the possibility of a happy marriage; she just feels things have gotten in the way. "Once the boys are part-time stepchildren again, I know things will settle down." Their ability to imagine a happy future shows that Marc and Linda still feel hopeful —that they both have a belief in a better future. There is tremendous power in positive thinking.

Can you recall your past together fondly, warmly, nostalgically? Do you enjoy traveling down memory lane? Were there cherished moments, good times? Good feelings? Was there once something between you? Was sex exciting? Does the thought of how good it used to be turn you on?

Changing does not mean you must go backward and restore old times. But a shared history of caring is a necessary foundation for growth. It's easier to make a marriage better, if it once *was* better.

Marc and Linda think fondly of their past. As Marc recalls, "We felt strongly about each other very quickly. It was even a little embarrassing—two mature people acting like kids. One friend even gave us an old 45 record, 'And They Called It Puppy Love.'"

Marc's and Linda's thoughts are just one way a couple might respond to these questions. George and Helen (pages 84–98), for instance, have very different responses to the first two questions. George and Helen feel stuck in a rut and neither could conjure up a fantasy of brighter days. As George says, "I think we're both sick to death of all the bickering, but, frankly, it's been going on so long between us, it will never change."

But as for the second question, both George and Helen could recall their past positively—and with ease. Helen remembers, "George's gentleness and kindness were the things that attracted me most. And even with all my complaints I know he's a truly good-hearted man. I think that's why he's such a good father. Our children knew they could always go to him." And George? "Helen was a go-getter. She appealed to me because I could see us getting a lot out of life together. I have fond memories until the kids got into high school. We were a really close family till then. My favorite snapshot is of the four of us on the bow of a boat about to go under Niagara Falls. The only things sticking out of these enormous yellow rain slickers and hats are our four happy faces. It was a wonderful trip."

Your answers will be different from those of Linda, Helen, Marc, or George, or any of the other couples. Each partnership is unique, and within each partner lie the resources for change and growth. As you uncover the strengths of your relationship, you will feel stimulated to start the quest for change.

> If your husband's role could be recast, can you conceive of him as a friend? Do you have any men friends who are like your husband?

Two married people can share no stronger bond than the potential for friendship. If you can see your husband as your friend, he is a man you believe has your best interests at heart.

Despite their differences, Marc and Linda feel a bond of friendship; they have good will toward each other. But a sense of friendship can vary. Though Helen doesn't see George as an ultimate choice of a friend, she admits to feeling comfortable with him, "like an old shoe."

Chris and Sarah, despite their struggles marching to the beat of a different drummer, share a totally deep and abiding friendship. Their friendship has grown over the years: both agree that there really isn't anyone they'd prefer to be with more than each other. As Sarah comments, "If I had to pick a best friend, it'd be Chris." At the other extreme lies Ruth. Her anger and humiliation makes friendship with Dan inconceivable. "Men? Who needs the aggravation?" is her refrain. "Dan uses women. The notion of a woman as a person, a friend, an ally—not an object—is completely alien to him. I can't see him being my or any woman's friend." Friendship is a weak link between Ruth and Dan; for a couple like Chris and Sarah it is a critical tie.

> Imagine a difficult event, a trying time, an accident, a tragedy befalling you. In a crisis would your husband come through? Would you come through for him?

If you still feel you can count on each other, you must still care about each other. As long as these sentiments exist—no matter how tenuous—you have something to work with.

As troubled as Ruth and Dan's marriage may be, Ruth knows she would come to Dan's aid in a crisis. "Sure, I've walked out on him and he's run around, but strangely enough—don't ask me why—we haven't backed out till now and I don't think we'd fall apart in a crisis. In fact, I sometimes have imagined that a really serious 'outside' problem would bring us together, make us closer. It would give Dan a perspective—let him see how important our marriage is to him, how important I am to him. He's said it often enough. Maybe that would make him believe it."

Unlike Ruth, Helen doesn't have to use her imagination. "When you've been married as long as we have—death, illness, money problems—you've seen it all. And George has never been anything but decent and honorable—a real rock."

> Do you believe in marriage? Is it important for you to stay married, to be married? Do you think being married is preferable to being single? Do you want to preserve your relationship?

Desire, determination, and conviction reflect your commitment to the essential worth of your relationship. While you can't simply wish things better, having the desire to make things better makes change possible.

A belief in marriage, even when it is pragmatic rather than ideological, can be a binding force. Barbara, married to Steve, the man who always "fails" her, expresses the practical advantages of their commitment to marriage with biting humor, "Sometimes when I lie in bed next to him my only regret is that I don't have a large cast-iron pot to bash over his head. And then the only thing that stops me from getting up to fetch one is the thought that I'd be back on the single scene again. God spare me such a fate. When I think of the 'available' men (and the hordes of women after them), I start thinking that marriage—even to Steve —is the lesser evil."

Linda and Marc view the ties of their marriage with more lofty sentiments. Both are strong advocates of commitment and family—and the fact that this is Marc's second try only strengthens those convictions. As Linda recalls, "Marc has always said his divorce made him more, not less, committed to marriage."

Are you able to find each other likable?

It is important to be able to derive pleasure from a partner—even if only occasionally. Two people who can still laugh together, take joy in the same moment, are probably still emotionally bound.

For Anthony and Cindy, there can be real swings in their feelings. In the calmer periods, usually when they are distant from their families, they are both much better able to like each other. Marc and Linda find it difficult at this point to derive pleasure from each other. "Our relationship has deteriorated badly. Tension is always in the air," Marc explains. "I don't think we've had a lighthearted evening in months."

Chris and Sarah, by contrast, make love, take walks, take pleasure in their family together. There is a reservoir of good times and good feelings.

Do you trust your husband?

Trust is a fundamental connection in a marriage: it is the raw material upon which you can base a renewed relationship. It is not easy for you to maintain trust in your husband since conflict often serves to alienate you from each other. By recalling the trust you once felt, you can start to rebuild faith in each other. Mutual trust is an essential element in negotiation—you can't negotiate with a man you can't trust.

Do you have a mutual investment in someone, something, or some ideas? Are any of these your shared sentiments?

We make a good team.
Our business depends on our being together.
We couldn't do it to the family.
It's our second marriage and we have to make this one work.
Divorce is against our religious conviction.
We have to try for the sake of the kids.
We can't see the future without seeing us together.
If we don't work things out with each other, we'll end up in the same spot with someone else.
We want to have children together.
The single life doesn't have any appeal.
We know what's out there, and we think at least we have something going.
Marriage is sacred.
Life is only complete if you have someone with whom to share it.
God meant us for each other.
We can't see anyone else living in this house.

If you and your husband subscribe to any of these sentiments, you both probably feel that you *have* to and *want* to stay together. Belief in the importance of these sentiments can help you work to stay together—but only if these reflect your honest convictions. If these are merely excuses or statements of fear, not deeply felt values, they will not support your commitment to make your marriage succeed.

Marc, for example, feels very strongly about family, home, and community—these are the organizing principles of his life. These feelings strengthen his determination to make his marriage last. Linda does not have as strong feelings in these areas, but she respects Marc's sense of tradition. A man and a woman need not have identical convictions. As long as their beliefs and ideas are complementary, they can work together to achieve what they both want.

Shared values form the strongest bond for George and Helen. They both view themselves as needing to be married; they value the eighteen years they have shared. Their children are a very important link. As Helen says, "Maybe our kids are grown but we still see ourselves as a family. We've seen several long-term marriages fall apart, and I'm sure we've both toyed with the idea, but neither of us has this modern feeling, 'Okay, it's not working, let's get a divorce.'" In some sense their lives are so interdependent that both Helen and George could not see themselves alone. As Helen comments, "Call it social pressure, force of habit, who knows, but it would be ridiculous for George and me to be single."

By contrast, Debra and Scott don't share this sort of solid foundation. Debra feels, "We've lived together but we don't feel like a family. I think both of us sense that we can bail out. It's funny, but I think saying 'I do' does make a difference." For Debra and Scott, the desire to stay together is supported, ironically, by the parental pressure to break up: neither Scott not Debra want to feel as if they've succumbed to social pressure about their age or other differences. Debra also has another strong personal sentiment. "I really want this to work. I'm not quitting. At my age and with my past, I can't afford to."

Pressure, whether internal or external, makes success likelier. It is an attitude that supports your commitment to make things work.

Everyone has an idea of who's responsible for marital discord. Think of your marriage as a round circle. If you were to divide the circle to indicate how this responsibility was divided between the two of you, which would you choose?

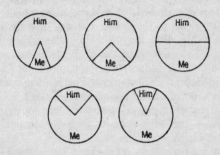

It may surprise you to learn that feeling responsible, or at fault, or guilty about your marriage is a positive sign. Unfortunately, guilt has gotten a bad name. But in proper proportion, guilt can be an indispensable motivator of your desire to change. Guilt reminds you of your responsibility and of other people's needs. It reminds you that marriage is a two-way street.

If you don't see the difficulties in your marriage as "your" problem (as well as "his"), you may be reluctant to try to change. You'll expect him to do the changing. If you're sure it's all his fault, you're more likely to give up on your marriage. Reactions run the gamut: Barbara staunchly believes "It's all Steve's fault—he can't do anything right," while Sarah blames herself, "I know my trying to climb the career ladder at this point in our life is difficult for Chris and the kids."

Is there sexual interest and pleasure?

Orgasm alone is no basis for a relationship. But, if sexual attraction and excitement exists, most likely feelings do too. If you still find your man physically appealing, your relationship may still be viable.

Linda and Marc continue to feel sexual pleasure together, but sex does not solve all their problems. Linda explains, "Marc and I fit together. We can make wonderful love, then wake up in the middle of the night and do it all over—but not when we're irritated. We both don't let go of bad feelings in bed." Sex cannot bridge the gap for them; it's subject to the ups and downs of their now volatile relationship. But, they do enjoy lovemaking. They are still attracted to each other, and probably care as well.

And after a long-term marriage, how does sex unite Helen and George? Helen may tell herself she doesn't want it, but her body still responds to George's touch. And George, even when piqued, wants to make love. In spite of themselves—and sometimes to their consternation—they still find sex highly pleasurable.

Even for a short-term relationship lovemaking is an important tie. For Debra and Scott, sex can be terrific. As Scott jokes, "We have the best of both worlds. I've got a continual hard-on and Debra knows what to do with it."

Do you like yourself? Do you both feel worthwhile?

When two people feel they deserve better, when they believe they're entitled to greater happiness, they can create a spirit of mutual commitment to grow. Shared self-esteem is essential. It is a statement of personal optimism: things can change and we are worth it.

A troubled relationship can eat away at your self-esteem. Ruth and Dan are particularly vulnerable. Their relationship is volatile, angry, tense. Dan looks to other women to confirm his sense of self-worth.

Conflict can drag a couple down. Marc appears secure but can easily be undermined by criticism. And since this is his second marriage, he occasionally wonders, "Do I have what it takes?" Linda, when she doesn't receive the reassurance she needs from Marc, loses sight of some of her feelings of self-worth. But both think well enough of themselves to feel they deserve better.

For Brad and Jean, self-esteem has become an issue. Jean feels she has lived in Brad's shadow. Now that she is getting her chance in the sun, she is discovering that she *is* likable. Brad, who rarely stops to examine himself, would probably find the question a perplexing one. But if he took the time to examine his feelings, he would conclude that he feels worthwhile.

Not all couples are equals in this arena. Scott's self-esteem isn't an issue. Debra's is. Her lack of self-esteem is her undoing. Feeling badly about herself undermines a belief that happiness can ever be hers.

Are there feelings of love?

Linda and Marc still feel love for each other. Linda acknowledges, "In the rare quiet moments, we can feel a surge of emotion for each other. I love Marc and he loves me, but our fear is that if things don't change soon, love won't be enough to keep us together."

To be a significant tie, love doesn't necessarily have to be burning passion or intense desire. As Helen expresses it, "I don't think we were ever madly in love. But there's no question that for all our bickering and complaints we're comfortable with each other and we care. For me that's what love is."

In a volatile relationship extremes of emotion may make you feel love wax and wane. Barbara and Ruth are two women who sometimes forget what love is only to feel it intensely and passionately at other moments. But it is still there.

Love cannot be neatly defined. For you, love may be a special romantic sense, or a transcendent feeling of being beyond time, space, and your own body, or a calm, comforting sense of attachment. However you interpret love, it is crucial that you ask yourself, "Do we love each other?" Even if you can't put your feelings into words, your belief that love exists shows that your relationship still has possibilities, that there is a foundation you can build upon together.

AN IMPORTANT QUESTION OF A DIFFERENT KIND

In determining marital negotiability there is one important but unpleasant question that must be asked. This question is not meant to help you restore positive feelings about your marriage, but rather to help you realistically confront a situation that makes any attempt at change impossible.

Does staying in a partnership put you (or your children) at risk? Is there violence, physical abuse, suspicion of incest, child molestation, alcoholism, drug addiction, gambling, sexual abuse?

When these behaviors *continue* to exist, when they are not stopped, a relationship is NOT NEGOTIABLE. No partnership can be worked on when the well-being of one of the partners is in jeopardy. There are instances where destructive behavior comes under control. However, this *never* happens unless there is special intervention (for example, professional help, Alcoholics Anonymous, legal restraint). Without these interventions, a violent or abusive partnership can *never* change. If you accept promises ("I swear this will never happen again"), you are indulging in self-deception. Believing you can work on this alone, that things will get better without outside intervention, is a self-defeating and often dangerous delusion. Nothing can get better between two people until destructive behavior is brought under control.

No matter how good the intentions, you cannot work on a relationship where either partner acts destructively. By contrast, a partner who seeks professional help for these behaviors makes a satisfying marriage a real possibility.

Now that you've answered the questions, where do you stand? If uncovering the strengths of your relationship has shown you that your marriage is worth the effort and you decide to go on, to take your developing insights and put them to work, the next section demonstrates a variety of ways to actively apply the insights you've gained.

Now, where do Marc and Linda stand, for example? There's no question that the legacy of Marc's first marriage—an ex-wife, her medical career, alimony, Cary and Jonathan, joint custody, child support—stresses their partnership. Perhaps conflicts would not have occurred, or not as quickly, if this were a first marriage. But it isn't. Acting as if the past will go away won't work. But dealing with the present through an understanding of each partner's psychology and needs will. It won't change reality, but it will help Marc and Linda deal with reality maturely. Can they do it? Most probably. A strong foundation of feeling still supports their partnership. Yet both recognize the erosion of hope, the unrelenting tension. Timing is critical. To delay facing the issues is to risk frustration so intense that as Linda aptly says, "Love won't be enough."

Marc and Linda have the foundation of positive feelings that makes negotiation possible. But perhaps you have regretfully—in the wake of this evaluation—decided there is nothing left, that the only solution left to you is to dissolve your unhappy relationship. Will you accomplish anything by reading on? Absolutely! What we have learned about human nature is that no matter where and with whom you go, you take yourself and your unresolved feelings along. Without making an effort to understand yourself, you will invariably, inevitably reenact your mistakes. If you fail to understand your past, your own personal history, you will undoubtedly repeat it. So while you may have little or no investment left in a partnership, you should not abandon your commitment to understand yourself. If you continue to explore, to examine your needs, you offer yourself the possibility that your next connection will be truly different, and certainly more gratifying.

PART FOUR

Negotiating a Loving Relationship: A New Language of Love

"You don't declare bankruptcy with assets like ours."
—Helen

If you've decided your marriage can be saved, it's time to get to work. But negotiating may not sound like a very romantic way to restore love and satisfaction to your relationship. *Negotiating* and *loving*—the words don't seem to belong together. *Negotiate* conjures up images of lawyers in smoke-filled rooms, power brokers striking deals. But negotiation is also the foundation of the world of diplomacy, where people confer with one another to bring about agreement, accommodation, and understanding that restore harmony. The important difference here is that you and your husband are both on the same side. It may not sound romantic to have to work on our intimate connections, but in order for love to survive, we often have to be inventive, creative, resourceful. After all, there's nothing romantic about being miserable.

In the course of this book, you have developed insight into your relationship—its risks, its strengths, your needs, and your partner's needs. Now is the time to put your new insights to work. You may be feeling anxious at the thought of change. Countering your needs, changing your pattern is not only difficult and demanding but also frightening. Why is it so traumatic to give up these old ways, to relinquish your old need? After all, your pattern offers no real satisfaction. Why, then, do you keep it? Why do you perpetuate it?

You hang on to your conflict because it offers something fundamental: security. Even if your partnership is unfulfilling, it is predictable—stable, reliable, and consistent. Your need for security is a powerful force; it is a need you learned early in your childhood. All children are vulnerable, easily overwhelmed by the unfamiliar, the unpredictable. Early on they learn to reduce these anxious feelings by keeping to the familiar and avoiding change. When we become adults, we still fear the unknown, we still fear becoming vulnerable. So as painful as your marriage may be, it's a refuge from the anxiety of change.

Take Marc and Linda. Their arguments, dissensions, and troubles keep them unhappy but in familiar territory. Marc can sit back and label Linda selfish; Linda can bemoan her fate of living with a demanding man. Time after time each partner's perceptions are confirmed. The status quo continues. Dissatisfactions may mount, but anxiety is kept at bay.

This drive to reduce anxiety, to make yourself secure, exerts a forceful pull, so that protecting yourself is your first priority, rather than remaining open to change. With this attitude of "safety first," your decisions, your actions, and your partnerships suffer. With this control, there are no surprises and nothing to throw you off balance. No risks. No chances. Security! This is the big trade-off. You gain security and control by giving up curiosity, flexibility, freedom, and the happiness of a truly gratifying relationship. Given the emotional safety that this security provides, it takes real courage to abandon a pattern, to understand need and to attempt to change.

It is no wonder, then, that people ignore or run away from conflicts, split up and divorce, rather than attempt to negotiate. However, trying to run from anxiety is unfortunately no answer. Simple fact: no matter where you run you take yourself along. Even if you seek a different partner, it is only a matter of time before your conflicts will resurface. So while it is difficult and disturbing to confront yourself, it is, in the long run, the only way out. What's more, it works!

Now is the time to stop running away. We have developed a four-step negotiating plan that provides specific strategies to show you and your partner how to communicate with each other instead of withdrawing, how to make contact instead of remaining isolated, how to find neutrality instead of anger.

I. Create the Atmosphere for Special Meetings
II. Recall the Strengths Out Loud
III. Clarify Expectations
IV. Learn a New Language of Love

I. CREATE THE ATMOSPHERE FOR SPECIAL MEETINGS

Communications is the essence of negotiation. But you have to establish ground rules in order to make communication possible. You have to create the right atmosphere for your discussions.

Set aside special times to meet.   Negotiations work best in an ideal setting, separate from your everyday life. Choose a time and place associated with pleasurable feelings: in a favorite restaurant, after a good movie, in a bath together, during a weekend without the kids, on Sunday morning in bed, at a ski lodge with just the two of you, during a summer picnic. Change your environment. The more you make it different from your everyday world, the more relaxed you'll feel.

Marc and Linda went back to the café where they had had their first date. As Linda recalled, "Over wine, I looked at Marc and started to remember just how much I'd been attracted to him. Good feelings definitely make a difference—they reminded me how much I cared." Restoring good feelings, even in a limited way, may offer you and your partner hope that gets lost in everyday tension.

With the complications of modern life, it takes effort to create an atmosphere. It is difficult but essential—not only the first time, but all the times you meet to talk. Don't underestimate the importance of surroundings; a change of environment can help foster a change of perspective.

Keep meeting regularly. Consider your first encounter one of many. One exchange, no matter how successful, will never bring about meaningful or lasting change. *Continuity is essential.* Set up neutral times to be spent together regularly, and take care not to become sloppy, haphazard, or casual about your meetings. To demonstrate a commitment to growth, time together must be sacred. Excuses, delays, forgetfulness, missed rendezvous are the signs of self-sabotage. Letting them go unnoticed shows that one or both of you are feeling uncomfortable about direct confrontation. It is up to you both to prevent emotional discomfort from becoming an obstacle. Talk about not wanting to talk, be silent if that is your mood, but spend the time together.

Most people prefer to regard negotiating as having a time limit, but when you're hammering out an ever-changing, interpersonal relationship, not a two-year labor contract, there can be no time limit. Negotiating a partnership has no fixed, preplanned goal; it is a process of mutual exchange and growth. Setting a deadline is unnecessary, possibly damaging. It ignores the dynamic nature of emotional life. Negotiation is not a device to be turned on and off. It's a lifetime skill to be incorporated into your daily relations. It's a new style of communication. In fact, for some couples, this style of negotiating, this way of working out a relationship, becomes an ongoing aspect of their life together.

Never attempt to talk in the wake of an argument. No successful negotiation can begin in the heat of battle—so don't even try. If you are susceptible to the urge to keep battling it out, make a conscious effort to restrain yourself. Remember that you can take up your complaints in your regular meetings.

Keep things open-ended.   Your only goal should be open exchange and dialogue. People spend years watching problems develop, and then expect instant solutions. Do not expect to find answers and conclusions at each encounter; this creates pressure and ignores the fact that your problems have a history. If you maintain an attitude of "to be continued . . .," you are recognizing that a relationship is dynamic, ever-changing. Focus on the future, on the ongoing nature of your marriage. Open-endedness is an important reminder that resolutions may be difficult, elusive, time-consuming. Marc made a particular try at keeping things moving. "Before we sat down, I'd literally give myself a pep talk, 'Marc, it took you thirty-eight years to get this way. It'll take more than an hour to get things sorted out.' It didn't always work but I think it helped make me a little more tolerant."

Set limits to discussion time.   Ironically, once these encounters begin, a couple often feels an irresistible urge to talk and keep talking any time and any place. Resist this temptation except during your special times together. Why? Such talk can dilute the effect of a meeting ("I have nothing left to say to you") or aggravate a situation ("I don't want to hear another word about it"). To avoid these difficulties, put limits on your encounters. In fact, setting limits often helps reduce tension. "Once Marc and I had a forum, the dinner table didn't have to be our boxing ring. If we started getting angry, I could remind him that we'd work on it. It helped. The kids' complaints about my cooking started to feel different. They weren't the problem. They were a symptom of our problem—one we were working on. It even affected the kids. They sensed they couldn't provoke us to take sides. It had a calming effect on them too." Day-to-day difficulties can be viewed from a different perspective when they don't have to be hashed out and argued over the very moment they occur.

Don't involve third parties.   Talk to each other—and *only* each other. Don't get others to side with you; don't go public with your complaints. Best friends, mothers, in-laws are taboo. Why? Confidants of any variety inevitably become witnesses for the prosecution, taking sides, rendering opinions. Negotiations are not a trial set up to find a guilty party; they are attempts to create dialogue between two people. Remember, there is nothing easier than to gather sympathy from an outsider ("You poor thing, I don't see how you put up with it"), but other people's opinions can distort yours. Be blunt with people, if necessary, to prevent yourself from falling into this trap. Linda had to be. "My mother asked me if Marc's boys were difficult this past week. My response was quite a departure from what she usually hears from me; I politely told her that Marc and I were working on it and that I thought it best that she and I didn't hash it over. I could hear her voice drop as if I had wounded her. But when I stopped replaying my problems with her, I realized how my mother's well-meaning calls had always added fuel to my fire." Setting up these boundaries also serves to reinforce a commitment between partners: "It's only us—we're in this together."

And there's another important reason to keep third parties out of your marriage. An outsider—parent, sibling, relative, friend—may have some investment in keeping your marriage in a state of turmoil. Surprising, but true. For example, a friend may feel jealous of your marriage and may consciously or unconsciously work to undermine it. A parent with his or her own unhappy marriage may harbor resentments that spill over into feelings about yours. It's complicated enough to work out your own problems; don't inadvertently complicate that task by having others dump theirs into your lap too.

Prohibit emotional blackmail. As negotiations take shape, one of the easiest traps to fall into is indulging in emotional blackmail—using newly gained, intimate knowledge of each other as ammunition. As you learn more about your partner's needs, you also learn more about your partner's sensitivities. The more that is revealed, the greater the personal vulnerability. Such exposure involves enormous risk taking. It can happen only if trust exists. When you use what you know to attack instead of to build, you damage this trust—sometimes beyond repair.

George and Helen are two people for whom emotional blackmail would be a temptation. They could easily use their understanding of their respective needs as ammunition. It isn't hard to imagine Helen, in a moment of anger, lashing out, "You said yourself that you can't make a woman happy—why should I expect it'll be any different with me."

And George, despite his laid-back disposition, is not beyond hurting Helen where she is most vulnerable. Not that he'd get caught up in cross fire with Helen, but at the right moment he'd zap her with a barbed one-liner. "You're not unhappy with your need—you love taking over."

Using emotional understanding destructively can have no place in negotiations. If Linda, knowing Marc's need, were to lash out, "The only way you can feel like a man is if you boss everyone around," or Marc were to retort, "You were always treated like a princess and you still act like one," they would be tampering with privileged information and defeating the whole purpose of their effort.

Emotional blackmail can have no place in your negotiations. The potential for success lies in unbroken mutual trust.

Call a moratorium during life crisis. When the external demands of life become too great, you lack the concentrated energy that negotiations require—the ability to focus on your internal emotional self. Negotiations cannot proceed when any major life event intervenes: death, illness, loss, separation, birth of a child, relocation, job change, remarriage of ex-spouse, custody battle, financial reversal, and so forth. Such circumstances need too much attention to leave adequate room for personal reflections. Once the situation has been dealt with (not necessarily resolved, but at least attended to), you can get down to work again. For example, Marc and Linda would have done best to give themselves some time after the boys moved in before they tried to work on their relationship. When you are contending with major life changes, you need a period of adjustment to develop coping strategies. After you have dealt with the stressful event, you will be free to attend to your relationship once again.

Suspend criticism.   Probably the most difficult task a couple can face is to suspend criticism, to listen openly without drawing conclusions, making judgments, blaming. Partnerships in trouble often revolve around nit-picking, bickering, finding fault. Realistically one could hardly expect either person to suddenly become nonjudgmental. But agreeing to "hear each other out" is essential in creating the atmosphere. Each partner needs to be heard without interference, interruption, commentary. Each partner must be free to communicate equally without emotional censorship.

While an attitude of acceptance is essential for negotiation, it will not happen immediately. It may be discouraging when this shift to mutual tolerance is not forthcoming. But the fact that partners may have trouble abiding by their own resolutions should not be grounds for giving it up. If need be each session must begin with a reinstatement of the commitment to outlaw criticism. Helen and George try— but don't always succeed—in thoughtfully hearing each other out. When they do falter, they admit to it and try again.

Helen: "I know I put down your comments last time. I've tried my damnedest not to criticize you."

George: "I've noticed it—unfortunately it didn't last."

Like someone trying to diet, George and Helen need encouragement—even when success is measured in small steps.

Not everyone will need to proceed exactly this way to create the atmosphere for communication. Though there are general steps to be followed, each couple, aware of their own emotional obstacles, can and should personalize their style of negotiation based on insight into their specific needs, wishes, and conflicts. This is the crux of the communication of negotiation. Negotiation is an approach to improving our lives together based on mutual understanding. As the psychological dynamics of every couple vary, negotiations must likewise be different. Together, you and your partner can create your own style of negotiation, your own atmosphere for communication.

Now the stage is set for true communication. In this atmosphere two people can learn to make love work.

II. RECALL THE STRENGTHS OUT LOUD

Even when two people decide that a relationship is worth working on, they often neglect to tell each other about those things they feel are worthwhile. Pointing out your partner's strengths may feel like an admission of weakness on your part. You must shake off this fear and begin to remind each other of the positives in your relationship. What is positive, pleasant, and rewarding about your shared life? What is it you love in your partner? (Going back to Part III will help you focus on the positives, from kids to sex.) Express these unspoken feelings —it will help strengthen bonds and create a feeling of goodwill.

Reminding each other of the good in your relationship helps put difficulties in perspective. You may have grown so accustomed to thinking of the bad that you find it embarrassing to talk of the good. But speak out now to show that you are important to each other. And continue to speak this way throughout the negotiation—both during your special meetings and in the course of your everyday encounters. You will be telling your partner that he has strengths, that you appreciate his good qualities; and you will be reminding yourself that he is someone worth caring for.

III. CLARIFY EXPECTATIONS

Every person begins a relationship with hopes, dreams, and expectations. You pile this heavy baggage onto your partnership, but rarely share these expectations with your spouse. In a troubled marriage, these unspoken wishes must be clarified. During your special meetings, explore what was anticipated, what promises were implied or inferred, how you envisioned the future, how things were to be different, why you chose each other.

Linda and Marc looked at some of their expectations. Linda acknowledged that Marc's age and success, and the security they implied, were important. She liked the way he knew his own mind. She expected that with a man like Marc her life would be trouble-free. Yet beyond her wedding and a fantasy of sharing a nice home, Linda realized she had not envisioned in any detail how their life would turn out. It was something she had never thought through.

Marc's expectations were markedly different. Unlike Linda, he has a very detailed picture of his future: Linda at home, another child or two, eventually his boys joining them. He saw himself coming home every night to a large, content family. What he loved about Linda was her sunniness, her smile. Linda made him feel that she'd go along with him, follow his lead. And it was important to him, Marc acknowledged, that Linda, attractive and bright as she was, would also make him look good.

Not everyone will, like Marc and Linda, bring their initial romantic expectations to a relationship. If yours is a relationship of long-standing, like George and Helen's, perhaps, your initial expectations may no longer be pertinent. Your wishes may have changed. Clarifying your expectations enables each of you not only to sense how near or far you are from fulfillment, but also to understand how similar or different your views are. Expectations are an unwritten contract. When they are unfulfilled, each partner feels the breach. It's only after you spend time spelling them out that you can work together to give each other what you desire most.

IV: LEARN A NEW LANGUAGE OF LOVE

Now is the time for a critical shift. It's here, right here, that old patterns can be broken and new ones established. How? By developing new and different ways of communicating—learning to speak "a new language of love." It isn't natural—in fact, what we suggest will sound stilted at first, even artificial. Frankly, it is just that. Artificial means humanly contrived, manmade. And that is where these communications skills come from—people. Professional people—like us and others—have devoted themselves to developing communication techniques to break our self-defeating patterns. A new language to break old emotional habits. The skills are specific—quite different from spontaneous and ordinary exchange. (So specific and different that we've even included an Appendix, to show how some of our other couples, snagged in their own marital gridlock, can rework their communication.)

As with any new "tongue," practice makes for fluent exchange. The special beauty about the approaches acquired here is that they can become a vital part of your relationship forever—and that can make all the difference.

When you've clarified what you expected from your marriage, it is time to evaluate what you have actually established. Your day-to-day arguments reflect the gap between each partner's wish and the reality of your relationship. Now in your meetings move directly into the particulars of your problem, as each of you candidly reviews complaints, discontents, dissatisfactions. (But remember, in a very new and different way. Not the way the complaints were stated earlier in the Marital Gridlock section.)

Change Accusation to Reflection. Begin by confronting the issues directly. You must both take care to keep this discussion from erupting into a series of charges and countercharges. How can this be avoided? Start by omitting the word "you" from the start of your sentences. Why? Comments that begin, "You are ____ (selfish, cold, stubborn)," carry the sting of an accusation and invariably create defensiveness. In addition, "You are" labels a partner and implies problems are his or her fault—hardly an attitude that leaves room for dialogue. How then should you discuss your complaints? Talk in terms of *how your partner makes you feel.* Your discussions must be thoughtful reflections, not simple accusations. This kind of exchange marks the real entry into negotiations rather than the rehashing of old arguments. How does it work? (We will use Marc and Linda here. But remember in the Appendix you'll find other couples illustrated.)

Marc might tell Linda:

Accusation: You . . .	*Reflection:* I . . .
Selfish bitch.	I experience you as selfish, not contributing your share when you don't take time for the boys.
You don't give a damn.	I feel as if you don't care about me.
You never have a good word for my kids.	I get infuriated when you criticize the boys, as if you're always pointing out my failures.

Or Linda might say:

Accusation: You . . .	*Reflection:* I . . .
You can't ever say no to those brats.	I feel jealous when you constantly say yes to the kids.
Are you made of stone?	It drives me crazy when you don't talk about our problems.
You jump through hoops for everyone—except me.	I feel as if you care more about others than me.
You only give a damn about your "good name."	I might be wrong but I think it's more important what people think of you than how I feel.

Putting "I" in these statements is not merely a grammatical change. This style enables you to change accusations into explanations: accusations can be denied or rejected, but explanations are likely to be heard. This self-reflective stance is critical for negotiation; it interrupts the cycle of charges and countercharges.

Being able to say, "I feel . . .," "I think . . .," "I experience . . .," "I sense . . .," shows you are willing to take responsibility for your situations. It allows your partner to respond to your feelings. "You are . . ." builds walls. "I am . . ." builds bridges.

Reflect Together on Your Needs. Just as your self-reflective statements will build bridges between you and your partner, they will also serve to connect you with your inner feelings, to help you understand your need. You will begin to see the major issues behind your complaints and how these issues are the product of your unconscious needs. By sitting together and exploring their marriage and their pasts Linda and Marc began to discern the major issues behind their complaints for Marc, concern over being criticized; for Linda, an expectation to be cared for. But we don't mean to suggest insight happens magically.

Making these connections takes assistance. After all, needs are hidden. That is just why we've offered you a view of eight different couples. Each is an opportunity to see the connection between marital conflict and the needs at work. Don't just read this book—use it! Take notes, reread it. Don't hesitate to go back to each couple. What may at first glance seem irrelevant, may later feel like a perfect fit.

As you make these comparisons it helps to consider whether any of these critical issues lies at the heart of your conflict.

Jealousy	Disappointment
Competition	Impulsivity
Control	Suspicion
Domination	Respect
Mothering	Perfection
Reliability	Self-esteem
Sharing	Sexuality
Neglect	Communication

Trust	Fear
Identity	Mutuality
Dependency	Abandonment
Unavailability	Aggression
Intrusiveness	Ego
Deprivation	Passivity
Abuse	Withdrawal
Narcissism	

Don't rush! Making these connections takes *time*! You might need a long series of meetings. But you'll have a head start if you identified closely with the needs, wishes, and conflicts of one of the couples in the Marital Gridlock section. As you and your partner compare your complaints to those of the other couples, you will begin to clarify your own pattern of conflict. (You may even want to draw a diagram of your pattern.) As you compare your pasts to those of the other couples, you will begin to understand just what your needs are. You may find yourself talking things out using these various methods of negotiation:

• Disagreements ("I don't think my need is . . .")

• Questioning ("Are you sure that I really make you angry, not hurt?")

• Repositioning ("That idea would never have occurred to me, but I'll consider it.")

• Disputes ("You sense this about me, but I don't.")

• Redefinition ("You feel as if I'm doing this to you, but I really mean something else by it.")

• Renunciation ("That's bullshit.")

Arriving at a shared insight into problems is no easy task. It is fraught with complications and setbacks. And though, occasionally, insight comes as a sudden, brilliant flash of light, you are more likely to inch along until both of you finally share a changed perspective about yourselves and each other. When you reach this juncture, you can embark on breaking out of your conflict—*interrupting the cycle of your needs*.

Until now, your negotiations have emphasized reflecting, thinking, questioning—not doing. But simply accumulating insight does not make for change. To achieve change, you must translate your insight into action.

Be Aware of Your Need. First each partner must develop an active awareness of his or her own needs. You must not allow them to slip out of awareness back to the unconscious recesses of your mind. Instead, you must continually acknowledge their existence and their impact on your relationship. Marc and Linda reinforce their awareness as follows:

Need	*Personal Awareness*
Marc:	
I have a need to be perfect, to control.	Now, when I walk into my parents' house and see how everything is just so, I can appreciate how perfection permeated my upbringing.
	When things don't go right with the boys and Linda, I remind myself that it's unreasonable to expect otherwise with stepfamilies. If it disturbs me so much, it must be my need at work.
Linda:	
I need to be totally loved and appreciated.	When Marc is short with me on the phone, I tell myself that he has demands at the office and that it's being supersensitive to take it personally.

I make myself read articles about children of divorce. I'm trying to gain perspective. The more I understand the boys' feelings, the less I feel that they're taking Marc away from me.

Learn to talk to yourself about your needs. Become sensitized to your reactions. Catch yourself in the act of responding to your needs. Now that you know how your heart beats, stop and feel it. Develop an awareness of your inner life.

Acknowledge Your Partner's Need. Once you are conscious of your own need, you can start to share your awareness. Use your heightened consciousness by acknowledging your partner's need. Let him know you understand what he is experiencing emotionally. Convey this critical message, "I understand the feelings you go through." Looking at Marc and Linda can illustrate how it can be accomplished.

Understanding	*Acknowledgment*
Linda:	
Knowing Marc's sensitivity to her comments on his indulging the boys, she can help him see that a different point of view is not a personal criticism.	"When I ask you not to buy more things for the boys, I think you may feel as if it's a personal attack. Actually, I'm only trying to suggest that limits are important for kids."
Marc:	
Sensing that his involvement at work can trigger Linda's feeling uncared for, he can make clear there is no connection between the two.	"You might feel that my working late means I don't care about you, but it's only the burden of supporting five people that keeps me at the office."

The message conveyed by both partners is one of empathy: "I understand and respect your need. I care." This approach defuses tensions. When you understand each other's motives clearly, you do not interpret actions through the prism of your unconscious needs. Once you describe an intention explicitly, there is less room for your partner to misread it based on the distortions created by his need.

This openness in communication doesn't end the problem. Achieving solutions takes a great deal of time, as well as self-control—thinking things through, rather than acting out impulsively. Acting on impulse perpetuates conflict. It's like learning a new language—the language of communication.

Let's not fool ourselves. A couple struggling with conflict is going to find this new sort of communication artificial. It is. You're more accustomed to acting out your feelings than to thinking them through and verbalizing them. Utilizing this new language of negotiation starts to resolve problems.

Master Your Own Need.   You can defuse your need by being able to admit to your partner how your need makes you vulnerable or sensitive to your partner's actions. This candor, which you may find difficult to express at first, can alert your partner to the impact he has on you. Mastering your own need by being open can change the way your partner responds to you. There's no question that laying it all out on the table is risky. No one relishes the thought of such vulnerability. But if each of you admits your personal sensitivities, you will be taking a giant step toward understanding and growth.

As Marc noted, "I found myself getting uncontrollably angry when Linda told me Jonathan had no place sleeping in our room after one of his nightmares. But what I was able to do was to let her know that her tone of voice made me feel like a little schoolboy being reprimanded. Admitting my sensitivity to criticism wasn't very easy; but there was a payoff. Linda could then understand the effect she was having on me that wasn't even related to the issue of Jonathan and his nightmares. Once we sorted out our feelings, we could actually end up discussing my boy and the problems of stepchildren in a pretty neutral way."

While this openness in communication doesn't end problems, it can enable people to clarify what is really going on between them. Linda also found this to be true. "I think until we really openly acknowledged our needs to ourselves and each other, they kind of contaminated any problem we tried to sort out. Maybe I'm not less sensitive about attention, but I can put those feelings in perspective. Now I can say to Marc, 'Listen, I miss your phone call from the office because when you're so caught up in other things I feel unloved.'" Being able to express your vulnerability to your partner shows you have achieved a later stage of negotiation. It is a sure indication that the healing process is under way, that mutual trust is growing.

Withdraw from the Fray. Even when needs are well understood, it is impossible—and ridiculous—to expect that every moment of potential conflict can be calmly worked through. Insight doesn't erase your emotional responses to each other; it only makes them more manageable. To expect you to be totally controlled in all your reactions would reduce meaningful exchanges to absurdities. "I spilled the milk." "No, I spilled the milk." "No, no, I spilled the milk."

So what should you do when emotions are running high? Remind each other of your commitment to negotiation, and meanwhile withdraw from the fray.

How might this work to help Linda and Marc defuse their tension? The spaghetti dinner fiasco could proceed quite differently once they recognized the meaning of their reactions. Either Linda or Marc might point out, "Listen, don't you think there's more to this than just a bowl of spaghetti? I think we're getting caught up in the same old struggle with our needs. Let's work on it at our next talk."

Had they had enough distance, Linda or Marc might even have said, "What the hell—let's eat Chinese." After a while, withdrawing from the fray allows you to take even your own anger a little less seriously. You may even find it possible to introduce humor to defuse the situation.

The message, "I'm not going to get into this; let's handle it later," doesn't resolve a problem but puts it on hold till the time and mood is right for work. Emotions can't be shut off instantly, so postponing dialogue until anger and hurt have subsided prevents the escalation of hostilities. You will be actively refusing to get caught up in your needs, consciously deciding not to allow them to be played out once again.

Gratify Your Partner's Need.   An important way to interrupt your cycle of conflict is by responding positively to your partner's need. You must understand what is emotionally important to your partner and gratify that demand. This can reduce the friction that arises when two people unconsciously resist giving to each other.

Knowing Marc's sensitivity about control, Linda might reassure him in that area. Perhaps after the hectic Christmas day when Marc had ferried the children from one home to the other, she might comment, "I missed having you to myself today, but I think your effort to try and make everyone's holiday pleasant was quite a feat."

In the same situation, Marc might have positively responded to Linda's need for caring, "I'm taking the day after Christmas off and we'll have the holiday together— even if it is a day late."

By their actions, Marc and Linda are consciously doing something to satisfy the other's need. An attempt to fulfill your partner's innermost longings, to connect with your partner's private emotional world, is enormously reassuring. You are clearly expressing the desire to reach out to each other.

Don't miss the point of this suggestion by concluding that becoming nicer to each other is what we are advising. Becoming a "good guy" is not the goal. In order for these responses to be meaningful, they must be more than token gestures or attempts at appeasement. Your responses must be rooted in insight and empathy. It isn't that you simply capitulate to your partner's need, but rather that you learn to respect the importance it plays in his emotional life. This capacity for empathy allows for the real give-and-take with no strings attached. It reflects compromise, the hallmark of a mature relationship. When you both have arrived at the point where you are able to respond to the one you love because you have grown to understand him or her, you have truly negotiated a loving, satisfying relationship.

KNOWING IT'S BETTER

The process of getting what we want and deserve from our marriage takes each of us down a different path. We know things are better when we take time and listen to our own inner voice. Perhaps these will be your words.

We're less irritable with each other.
These days, I look forward to coming home.
We're managing the in-law situation.
The children seem calmer.
He's much more attentive.
We talk more.
Impotence is less of a problem.
He goes to AA regularly.
I can tell him when I'm angry.
I've lost interest in having an affair.
We do more as a family.
I know he loves me.
At home he's pulling his own weight.
We haven't threatened divorce in months.
Finally I feel appreciated.
We're friends again.
He's learning to respect me for what I am.
We've stopped any physical abuse.
I'm learning to be my own person.
I can tell him what turns me on.
We've decided we want a baby.

If we work to understand ourselves and our marriage, each of us in our own special and particular way will hear the inner voice say, "Yes, I know it's better."

INTIMACY

Though this is clearly a book about marriage, it is also a book about intimacy. So we'd like to leave you with the image of Rosa "dancing" gently to the swing music in her father's arms. And the reminder that while there isn't one particular way to achieve it, well-being *is* forged in the arms of another person.

Our hope is that this book may help couples begin to remove obstacles that prevent their intimate connections. Marriage, a good marriage, with all of its complexities, offers us the best possibility of intimacy. Taking what is possible and making it real is what each of us longs for and each of us deserves.

APPENDIX

More on a New Language of Love

We've already said that speaking a new language of love is not something that comes automatically or spontaneously. Since that is the case we thought it useful to illustrate how three additional and very different couples—Helen and George, Sarah and Chris, Debra and Scott—learned to communicate. The choice is intentionally limited to three. We want, as always, to offer ideas and guidelines, but not ready-made solutions. We think it more useful to leave you wanting to learn more rather than believing you've learned all there is to know. Frankly, we also thought detailed example after detailed example could get tedious and over-done. So we opted for three. Your having these "extra opportunities," we hope, will stimulate your own thoughts and ideas. As always, we believe that with the right direction every person has what it takes to get what he or she deserves out of marriage.

A NEW LANGUAGE OF LOVE FOR HELEN AND GEORGE

Needs:

Helen: To rely on no one
George: To feel powerless

Changing Accusation to Reflection

To maintain this as an open discussion and prevent it from degenerating into an argument, Helen and George have to shift from accusing each other to reflecting. How would it actually sound?

Accusation: You . . .	*Reflection:* I . . .
Helen:	
You always manage to ruin the evening. If you don't fall asleep in the movie you find an excuse to leave early.	When you don't show interest in the things we do together, I feel as if I'm alone, as if I don't have anyone to depend on.
George:	
When it comes to sex you're an ice cube.	If you don't respond to me sexually, I feel frustrated and powerless.

Be Aware of Your Need

As the real unconscious sources of George and Helen's conflict keep emerging they can begin to develop ways of preventing their needs from coming between them. How can they disrupt their pattern? First by making a concerted effort to remain conscious of their respective needs.

Need	*Awareness*

Helen:

My need is to rely on no one.	Whenever I look at my father's picture I remind myself of how his death left me feeling—all alone. It finally makes sense to me why I have a need to trust no one.

George:

My need is to feel powerless, peripheral with women.	When I set out to do something for Helen I remind myself that at work I don't make mistakes. I literally repeat to myself: "If I screw up now it's because my need affects my relationship with women."

Acknowledging Your Partner's Need

Once partners can keep their needs conscious, a logical next step is to use this awareness with each other, integrating it into the everyday course of events. This means acknowledging a partner's need, letting him or her know you understand what he or she experiences emotionally.

Helen:

Aware of George's need, Helen can help him break the link between her behavior and his need.	It's not that you can't turn me on—you feel my breasts respond. But if I'm angry I don't feel like being close and I stop myself from giving in.

George:

George can help Helen understand the motive for behavior and therefore stop reinforcing Helen's need.	My leaving the party early may feel as if I'm walking out on you but the fact is that most people bore me. I'm really happy on my own—fishing.

This openness in communication doesn't end the problem. Achieving it takes a great deal of time and enormous self-control—and capacity to think things through rather than act out impulsively.

Mastering Your Need

If each person masters his or her own need—by being able to admit how a need makes us sensitive and vulnerable to our partner's actions—the need-based conflict can be defused.

Helen:

When the first thing you do after work is come home and turn on the TV, I feel hurt, as if you're turning it on and me off.

George:

I walk away from you when you raise your voice and sound irritated because you seem so sure of yourself; I feel as if I can never have any impact on you.

This emotional honesty based on self-knowledge can go far toward changing the way another person responds to you. Once achieved it is a sure indication of a healing process and growing mutual trust.

Gratifying Your Partner's Need

Eventually, you will be able to understand and accept your partner's need. At that point, you must do or say something that directly empathizes with your partner's sensitivity, a gesture that gratifies your partner's innermost feeling. How?

Helen, in a note George found in his lunch on one of his fishing trips:

"I will really miss you today. A Sunday without you is bleak."

George:

I know how you worry about being left on your own. Would you feel better if I increased my life insurance? I want you to feel taken care of.

In these sort of statements each person is reaching out and making an effort to be emotionally responsive. When we can arrive at this point with the person we love we have truly negotiated a modern relationship.

A NEW LANGUAGE OF LOVE FOR SARAH AND CHRIS

Needs:

Sarah: To find her own identity
Chris: To maintain the status quo

Changing Accusations to Reflection

Accusation: You . . .   *Reflection:* I . . .

Sarah:

You live in the Dark Ages. You act as if women should stay "barefoot and pregnant."	I'm struggling to get out from under and when you don't seem to support me I feel as if you're my enemy.
The next time you tell the kids they have a part-time mother I'll tell them because of you they won't have any mother at all.	I'm trying hard to be a good wife, mother, and professional, and your criticisms devastate me because I can feel so undermined.

Chris:

These days you don't give a damn about anyone but yourself.	When you include new things in your life I feel as if I'm being excluded. I guess the more room you make for other things the less I feel there is for me.
Keep telling me you're too tired for sex and I'll stop asking.	I read "too tired" as lack of interest in me. I lash out because I think I'm losing you.

Be Aware of Your Need

Need   *Awareness*

Sarah:

My need is to search for identity.	There is nothing like seeing Suzy, the star pitcher on my son's Little League team, to remind me of how my need took hold, how when I was a child life set limits on a girl's horizon.

Chris:

My need is to keep from losing the status quo.	On camping trips I love to cook. At home I hate it. The difference is my need at work. Now I realize that it is my need that keeps me struggling against an even give-and-take.

Acknowledging Your Partner's Need

Sarah:

Sarah can help Chris understand that her intent is to grow personally, not to upset him.

Because of work I am spending less time with you, but I'm much more satisfied as a person and in the long run I think that adds, rather than detracts, from our relationship. Deep down I think you know it's so too.

Chris:

Chris can help Sarah see his requests on her time aren't arbitrary demands.

It's not my intent to interfere with your career. I'm asking you to stay home because I'm lonely without you. I know you're caught between a rock and a hard place.

Mastering Your Need

Sarah:

If I think you're telling me what to do with my life, I feel as if you're my father insisting I behave like his good little girl and it infuriates me.

Chris:

I grew up believing in man and wife. You want us to be man and woman. In my head I know it's the right thing but it can feel all wrong.

Gratifying Your Partner's Need

Chris and Sarah are struggling in different ways to deal with the same social issue; therefore gratifying needs can be a truly joint effort. Together both partners can work toward the mutual reduction of stress.

Specifically it means being able to say to each other, "Look, these changes aren't easy for either of us, what can we do to eliminate or at least reduce some of the pressure?" Out of empathy solutions can be forged.

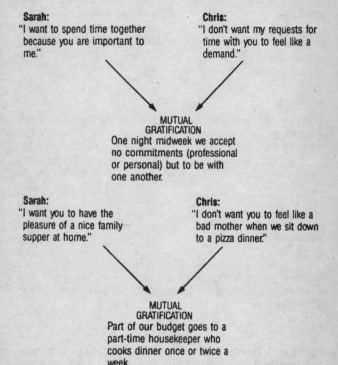

Sarah:
"I want to spend time together because you are important to me."

Chris:
"I don't want my requests for time with you to feel like a demand."

MUTUAL GRATIFICATION
One night midweek we accept no commitments (professional or personal) but to be with one another.

Sarah:
"I want you to have the pleasure of a nice family supper at home."

Chris:
"I don't want you to feel like a bad mother when we sit down to a pizza dinner."

MUTUAL GRATIFICATION
Part of our budget goes to a part-time housekeeper who cooks dinner once or twice a week.

The list of ways couples can mutually gratify their needs is dependent on the extent of their resources. There are many, including housekeepers, child care services, baby-sitters, after-school programs, camps, laundries, take-out foods, personal secretaries, home computers. Clearly these services can cost money. Not all have to. Child care can become a neighborhood cooperative. Baby-sitting can be exchanged between friends. A weekend marathon of family cooking can make a week of ready-to-eat meals. Dividing tasks between members of the family—including children—can improve the situation. Improving a marriage can be a family affair.

A NEW LANGUAGE OF LOVE FOR DEBRA AND SCOTT

Needs:

Debra: To test if she is loved
Scott: To satisfy a craving for love

Changing Accusation to Reflection

Accusation: You . . .	Reflection: I . . .
Debra:	
Why don't you pick up the towels, you lazy bastard.	When I spot something you've left on the floor I see red. It makes me feel the only value I have for you is as a servant.
I'm only a convenient fuck. You don't even know what makes me feel good.	When you make love without taking time to be tender, I feel as if I don't exist for you as a person.
Scott:	
Bitch, bitch, bitch.	Your barrage of complaints confuses the hell out of me. One day something matters, the next day it doesn't. I feel as if you're testing me not accepting me.

Walk out. See if I care.

When you threaten to break off it drives me crazy. It makes me feel as if I can't depend on your support. I can't take the unpredictability.

Be Aware of Your Need

Need

Awareness

Debra:

My need is to test if I'm loved for myself.

These days whenever I volunteer to help Scott with something, I stop and ask myself, "If he accepts my offer, will I end up feeling used?" It makes me understand that by constantly offering I set myself up to feel exploited.

Scott:

My need is to satisfy my craving for love.

When Debra's annoyed because I've left an empty milk container in the refrigerator, I visualize my father pointing to the car I just washed, furious at the half-assed job. It's obvious how I sabotage things to get attention.

Acknowledging Your Partner's Need

Debra:

Debra can help Scott stop unconsciously equating how much she does for him with how much she cares.

If I insist that you pitch in it's because I'm tired after work and need help—it has nothing to do with my caring for you.

Scott:

Scott can help Debra become less vulnerable to his behavior, less ready to assume the worst.	When you feel as if sex has been wham-bam-thank-you-ma'am, it's quick because you turn me on, not because I'm ignoring you or using you. With my last girlfriend I couldn't even get it up.

Mastering Your Need

Debra:

It takes very little to give me the sinking feeling in my stomach that if I stop working at things I'll lose you.

Scott:

I may sound like a little boy, but the smell of your banana bread when I come home makes me feel content.

Gratifying a Partner's Need

Can Scott connect with Debra? Can he gratify her need and help her feel loved for herself? Yes, provided he is continually reassuring. It may mean, for example, calling Debra each day at work. He must give her lots of attention —cards, flowers, notes, concrete expressions of his sentiments—not as a response to a demand but rather in response to his awareness of her fragility.

What will gratify Scott? Ironically, similar caring behavior from Debra. But Scott needs this sort of attention not to relieve an inner tension, but rather to create a pleasurable sense of well-being and coziness. Debra will have to give—but with no strings attached.

EPILOGUE

I think there's another way to see things. If people realized that relationships weren't paradise we'd be a lot better off. And in my mind since there's no such place on earth anyway not quite paradise seems like a great place to be.

—Bernie Kaplan, Doubleday sales representative, remarking on the title of this book

ABOUT THE AUTHORS

Bonnie Maslin, Ph.D., is a psychotherapist who holds a doctorate in educational psychology from New York University. Yehuda Nir, M.D., is an associate professor of psychiatry at Cornell University Medical College, New York, and is in private psychiatric practice. They are happily married to each other, and live in New York City. Maslin and Nir are also the authors of LOVING MEN FOR ALL THE RIGHT REASONS.